Angels

IDOLS

Angels

IDOLS

The Rise, Fall,
and Redemption of
a Would-Be Pop Star

REGIE HAMM

TATE PUBLISHING & Enterprises

Published by Tate Publishing & Enterprises, LLC
127 E. Trade Center Terrace | Mustang, Oklahoma 73064 USA
1.888.361.9473 | www.tatepublishing.com

Tate Publishing is committed to excellence in the publishing industry. The company reflects the philosophy established by the founders, based on Psalm 68:11,
"The Lord gave the word and great was the company of those who published it."

Book design copyright © 2010 by Tate Publishing, LLC. All rights reserved.
Cover design by Leah LeFlore
Interior design by Lynly D. Grider

Published in the United States of America
ISBN: 978-1-61663-440-7
1. Biography & Autobiography / Personal Memoirs
2. Biography & Autobiography / Entertainment & Performing Arts

10.04.30

Angels and Idols

DEDICATION

To my father, Ron; my mother, Diane; and my brother, Leny. You are the pillars of my past.

To my wife, Yolanda; my daughter, Isabella; and my son, Gabriel. You are the joy of my present.

To my heavenly Father, You are the keeper of my future.

And to all those families in the corners of the world who care for and love special needs children of all types. You are doing God's work, and you are not alone.

TABLE OF CONTENTS

OLD MAN AND IWO JIMA

I've heard the story since as long as I can remember. I can still see it being told in hushed and reverent tones around the leftover-laden tables of Christmas or Thanksgiving—the choking smoke of burning diesel and exploding artillery shells conjuring itself through the waft of pumpkin pie and cornbread dressing, the echoes of screams and ancient, urgent orders barked through the faint sound of a football game in the next room, the story of a young marine in the volcanic ash of Iwo Jima during World War II, having dug an uncommonly deep foxhole. According to the family legend, he just happened (through random events) to arrive at his forward position before the rest of his platoon. The others were possibly on some detail that held them back. He possibly got an earlier start. He might have been sent ahead of the platoon for some reason. We never really knew. The fog of war and haze of history have shrouded the intricacies of the moments in question. Those details have long since been buried in the graves of the fallen, but the heart of the story still beats inside of me. I believe my life was forever altered in 1945.

My grandfather, a man of average height, had dug a very deep foxhole in preparation for an upcoming battle. When the rest of the platoon arrived, one of his tall compatriots only had time to dig a shallow foxhole before all hell broke loose and the platoon began getting barraged with enemy mortar fire. The tall soldier yelled over to my grandfather, "Tice, switch holes with me! I'm too tall for this one, but you'll be fine in here. Please, Tice! I need a deeper hole; you don't need one that deep!" Watching the lanky marine trying to curl his oversized limbs and torso into undersized shelter, my grandfather agreed, and they rolled through intolerable waves of explosions and gunfire, past each other into the other's foxhole. As the man was crouching into his new position and throwing my benevolent, young grandfather a casual thank-you salute, the deep, well-dug foxhole was instantly incinerated with a direct hit by a mortar round. There was nothing left but scorched earth and fragmented body parts. Pawpaw Tice (as we called him) told my father in later years that he stared at the carnage for minutes, realizing that if he'd shown up ten minutes later and not dug so deep, the man would've never asked to switch. If that hadn't happened, it would've been my grandfather's remains smoldering on the sands of Iwo Jima and not the taller marine's. He said it always bothered him how random it all was. Random. He just happened to get there first. There just happened to be an uncommonly tall man in the next hole. That man just happened to ask him to switch holes. They just happened to switch in the nick of time. Random.

Thomas Tice, my grandfather, somehow survived two years on Japanese island battlefields—with untold random events that kept him alive, no doubt—came home to the United States, and produced the last of his four children: my mother. I can trace my entire existence back to one bloody, terror-filled night on an obscure island ten thousand miles away from my warm bed. I can see a hand of providence directing the path of a scared, tired, haggard marine through the muck and minutiae of war. Every day I've enjoyed on planet earth was born in a single, sweaty, adrenaline-fueled roll from one foxhole to another in some place I've never seen by someone I never knew in a time which I didn't live. God only knows the moments that changed everything to lead to that moment on Iwo Jima: the attack on Pearl Harbor, the American response, the global conflict that emerged with billions of moving parts that triggered billions of decisions, one of those decisions being a young Mississippi barber enlisting in the Marine Corps, his training and deployments, the convergence of events that led to the taking of Iwo Jima as a strategic military target and the bloody battle for that tiny piece of earth, the decisions that led to sending that young marine to that particular place in that battle and his decision to switch places at the last minute with another young marine, the ironic event that became an off-handed war story to a son-in-law, which became a holiday staple in my life, the legend that became the story you've just read and that will now alter something about you forever. God only knows the moments that change everything.

Random events. Life, to some, is a series of disconnected, random events—one giant pinball game where we are all tiny and pointless, careening into bumpers and dodging one another, hoping to score enough points to continue the kinetic roll. We tell ourselves that this moment doesn't have that much importance. It's just a Thursday. It's just lunch. It's just a date with the girl from English Lit. It's just a different foxhole. Will we remember it? Probably not. Will it have any lasting impact on our life? Who knows? We're always hoping to arrive at some magical moment of truth, a life changer, one of those moments that gives us clarity and epiphany. We think we'll know it when we see it or feel it. We are oriented through movies, TV, and dramatic novels to watch for the heavens to open and to listen for the angels to sing. Then we'll suddenly know something we didn't know before. We'll have new wisdom and new light and new purpose. Surely that moment isn't happening right now. This is just a regular day full of regular moments. Yes, our random lives can seem mundane and purposeless. The moments that course through the veins of our existence can feel uneventful and redundant. Random events seem to be happening to us all the time.

One such event showed up in my date book somewhere in the fall of 1992. A random series of events and a lifetime of coincidence had led me into the role of staff songwriter for a company called McSpadden Smith Music. Primarily a Christian-music-based publishing company, they were incredibly young and wildly successful. I was a newly married, twenty-something songwriter who was finding favor in the world of Christian music. I'd had a couple of minor hits on the radio and was starting to turn some heads. The future was bright and wide open. In those days, I was a bit of a workaholic. I would write songs all day, have dinner, and then write through the night into the wee hours. I would then go to the Vanderbilt University track, run a few miles, and then head home for a shower and bed only to start the whole routine over again the next day around eleven. Because I wasn't making much money as a writer, I would also take occasional odd jobs to bolster my income. I was going full speed. All out. I was certain that success was completely within my grasp and, more importantly, within my control. Shawn McSpadden, the owner of the publishing company, and I were constantly scheming and planning and working toward the goal. The goal? Success. Achievement. More songs written. More songs recorded. More songs on the charts. More songs topping those charts. Gold records. Platinum records. More money. More success. More, more, more. Get it done. Take care of business. Focus. Do what the other guy won't.

Start earlier. Stay later. Never be satisfied. Dig deeper. Do it better. Work as hard as you think you can and then work harder. That was the mind-set. I truly believed that with that work ethic, I had control over the destiny of my music and life. I was certain that with enough sweat and opportunity, I could make it happen. I kept my datebook full at all times.

My wife and I lived in a Spartan, 350-square-foot apartment above a small house in downtown Nashville. We paid three hundred bucks a month for it and lived in four rooms: front room, kitchen, bathroom, and bedroom. You could fit all our worldly possessions in the back of a pickup truck. We were built for speed. Three minutes to West End Avenue, five more to Music Row. Life was quick and spontaneous. We didn't do much of anything except sleep, work out, and work. We were determined to make it somewhere. We weren't sure where, but it was going to be great when we got there; we just knew it. So we worked. Days were a blur of meetings, writing appointments, business lunches, and being holed up in recording studios for hours on end. Nights were filled with industry parties and hanging out with the right people...and being holed up in recording studios for hours on end. I won't lie; it was a good time. The feeling of being young and taking the world by the horns is a powerful one. You feel invincible. You believe you're immortal. Though I was married to my dream girl and best friend, we didn't hang out with other married couples. All our friends were single. There wasn't much talk of children or school systems or health insurance or life insurance or home values or anything of that sort. Make the rent. Work hard. Play hard. That was the life we were living.

Amidst the swirling energy of that life, I befriended a young song plugger at McSpadden Smith Music. His job was to comb through the songs I was turning in, make copies of the ones he felt would work for certain artists, and pitch them to those artists. He was a thoughtful, soft-spoken soul named David Moffitt. David was quiet and deliberate. His perfectly groomed and parted red hair, button-down shirt, khaki pants, and glasses made him seem academic and astute. I would never have guessed he was a songwriter too. He didn't seem crazy enough. He was always on time. He appeared to be together and in control. He chose his words carefully and wasn't angry for no reason. In short, he was almost the exact opposite of me. I could never have known that he was protecting three ominous words that would change my life forever and haunt me in strange and frightening ways. Of all the publishing companies on Music Row, I had walked in to that one. I'd signed a contract with that one. I had been attracted to the pace and the action. I had hitched my wagon to what I believed was a shooting star. I'd signed with one of the youngest, hippest companies in Nashville in an attempt to become something, anything other than what I was. The thing I wanted the most was staring me in the face, yet an unlikely, mild-mannered employee of that young, hip company would hold the touchstone to my true purpose.

"Let's write a song sometime," he said casually one afternoon. "I have an idea I think you could really help bring to life." I wasn't sure what to make of writing a song with an employee of the company for which I was contracted to be golden. It seemed a little weird and unorthodox. Still, I was booking anyone and everyone, and I felt something interesting might come of it. So somewhere in the fall of 1992, a random encounter with the song plugger of a small publishing company in Nashville became a penciled-in appointment in my date book. Another writing session. Another song in a catalog full of them. Another melody. Another lyric. Another possibility of success. Another random attempt at making something special happen.

Certainly David couldn't have known that my favorite book

was Dickens's *Great Expectations*. He wouldn't have known the reasons for my being drawn to that story at age nine (the same year I started writing songs) and my deep connection to Pip, the main character. He couldn't have realized that I saw myself in Pip and his desire to reach beyond his embarrassing beginnings to something grandiose and important. He couldn't have known I had that same desire. He couldn't have seen the same undulating fear in my heart that pounded in Pip's—the fear that I would never truly rise above what I was, no matter how hard I tried. He couldn't have looked into my past and seen a five-year-old, self-taught prodigy playing gospel music in country churches and all-night singings. He wouldn't have seen my formative years and my family band singing in high school gyms and in mall parking lots, being laughed at by kids my own age, mocking the message of Christ and the down-home way in which my family delivered it. He couldn't have known I had spent my entire life running from church picnics and Sunday morning services into some place cooler and hipper. He couldn't have seen the raw ambition to get out of a world I considered to be a wasteland and reach the heights of some blinding success somewhere else. David Moffitt could never have known any of that, but the keys he held in the idea vaults of his mind would unlock the doors of my childhood and release the demons. The three words he was harboring for me would foreshadow the rise and fall of a would-be pop star, the destiny of a child not yet conceived in rural China, the meaning of an enigmatic genetic disorder that would devastate a family, and the redemption that would come from the rarest of places.

My chance encounter with David Moffitt was as random as two marines switching foxholes in the heat of a battle. But it was about to set the stage for the time of my life.

I SURRENDER ALL

The upstairs writers' room was windowless and sparse. In all my years of songwriting, it has always amazed me how writer's rooms get furnished, literally with the leftovers. If you're moving out of your first apartment and want to get rid of all that thrift store furniture you bought in college, or stuff you pilfered from the side of the road at three in the morning, take it all to a publishing company on Music Row and drop it off. They'll have all their writers' rooms furnished with it in a matter of hours. Our upstairs writers' room at McSpadden Smith Music was classic—an uncomfortable, secondhand couch (circa 1980-something), an out-of-place, rickety chair, and an-out-of-tune spinet piano were the only furnishings. There was a large, angled wall that served as a gray canvass for visiting writers to wax philosophic or funny or pithy upon with a Sharpie. It was interesting reading when you had played the same mundane chord progression for the eightieth time, waiting on lightening to strike it into genius. The floor was covered in nondescript blue, low pile carpeting. The usual suspects—stray guitar picks and pencils, a lone piece of obsolete audio gear in the corner, a typed lyric of some phantom song from some previous phantom writer from some previous, phantom writing session conspicuously residing on the piano music stand. This is the world in which songwriters live and breathe. This night and this room were no different.

I was early, which is unusual for me, and began tinkering on the piano. I began my musical journey as a drummer. I simply picked up a pair of drumsticks one night, sat at the drums in my father's church, and began playing along with my mother at the piano. I was five years old. Everyone watched and listened in amazement and dubbed me a wonder kid from that point on. I never took lessons or needed much instruction. I had a natural musical instinct. Throughout my teens I had begun applying that instinct to the piano and songwriting. By the time I was in my twenties, the piano was my closest friend. I wasn't classically trained and had never had a lesson, but I had learned how to make a pleasant noise on that instrument. It had become my stock and trade. I can usually tell within thirty seconds of putting my hands on the piano keys what kind of a day or night it's going to be. The instinct of composition is magical in some ways—the weight of the keys, the way the sound bounces off that particular room, the tuning level of the piano. What I just ate or drank will make subtle differences in my sodium retention and determine how nimble my fingers feel. If I've just gone on a long run and had lots of water, I'll play a certain way. If I've just inhaled a giant burrito and a half-gallon of soda, I'll play another way. All these variables are minute and microscopic, but they all factor in to where my fingers are going to land on a keyboard and how my brain and soul will react to what I hear. This particular night was going to be a ballad night. I could feel it from the jump. What I had eaten, what I was hearing in the room, how my fingers felt on the keys, all keeping me focused on a progression that kept presenting itself. I learned many years ago to always follow that voice, at least for a while. So I fumbled with C over B flat and certain melodies that occurred underneath that progression until David Moffitt arrived.

"Sorry I'm late," he said, walking in slowly. The usual reasons were given. Those reasons morphed into the infamous, perennial songwriter inside joke: writers' room small talk. It's a well-known fact that writers will often talk the entire session away in order to keep from having to actually write. Writers hate to write; they just love having written. Writing is one of the most intimate of tasks. All your insecurities and limitations are up close and personal. Songwriters, being some of the most insecure people on the planet, are faced with absolute terror in a new collaborative endeavor. Many writers (including myself) simply write off the first session as a get-to-know-ya session. I never expect anything to appear in a first-time collaboration. It takes the pressure off. So David and I talked and talked and talked. Finally, with a sly grin, he said, "I want to throw this idea out to you. What about a song called 'I Surrender All'?"

I had been raised singing the original, public domain standard and started playing it and singing it as a joke. "They did it already, Dave. You might have heard it; it's actually pretty good." We both had a laugh, and he said, "You know what I mean, revisit that title with a fresh approach."

"I'm intrigued. Sell me," I said. I was a bit unsure and skeptical, but he sort of straightened himself into his singing stance and crooned the opening strains to the chorus. "I surre...nder all," He put the stress in an unexpected place. It tweaked my ear, and I liked it. As he was singing, I placed my hands on the piano keys and began fumbling with the chord progression I had been playing before he arrived. It kind of worked seamlessly with what he was singing. How random is that? He smiled and said,

"Man, I like that little hook." That's when we knew we were onto something; we decided to press on and finish this happy little accident.

The process of writing can be an arduous slog through ideas and concepts and melodies and rhymes and everything you've experienced in your life to that point. Very often, it is temporary moments of inspiration surrounded by hours (sometimes days, weeks, or months) of mundane crafting. The process of writing "I Surrender All" was a perfect example of that. The first evening of writing was pure inspiration. We finished the chorus in its entirety that night. If I remember correctly, we also had the melody for the verses reasonably mapped out as well. It was a good night's work. I was feeling pretty good about the nuts and bolts of the song—strong idea, strong melody, strong hook, and strong chorus lyric. I left that night knowing I was in the middle of a nice piece of music. It felt good. I had been using my skills, knowledge of symmetrical melody construction, well-honed lyrical craft, intimate knowledge of what kinds of words made maximum impact in a song such as this, and knack for syntax and meter. I had not yet fully processed the concept, however. I had not really thought through the implications of making such a statement to God. It would take years before I would fully understand, embrace, and eventually live out my own words.

I surrender all my silent hopes and dreams
Though the price to follow costs me everything
I surrender all my human soul desires, if sacrifice requires
That all my kingdoms fall. I surrender all.

The notion of surrender has never been one to which I've taken kindly. My father often used me as an example of those Christians who cannot surrender to God's will. From the pulpit, he recounted hundreds of times the family Bible story. Being the master of exposition that he was, this fable of a two-year-old doing battle with a parent over control of the sacred pages of the family Bible was a priceless arrow in his quiver. After an hour or so of singing and playing to a church crowd and warming them up, my father would then ramp into his sermon. Every night of a six-night crusade, which is what we normally did, had a different theme. My father, an expert storyteller and anointed (for lack of a better word) preacher, would read a scripture and then expound on it for the next hour to hour and a half. Within the first moments, he would have every soul in the building in the palm of his hand. He did his research. He knew that the average attention span is just under three minutes. He knew exactly when to be funny, exactly when to be serious, exactly when to make a point, exactly when to be whimsical, exactly when to be frightening, exactly when to throw a thick, Southern accent and when to throw a thick northern accent, depending on the audience. In all my years of watching flashy, entertaining preachers bring down fire everywhere from tiny backwoods churches to large televised events, I never saw anyone do it better than my father. He swaggered the stage like a rock star. He had the confidence of an athlete and the persuasive power of a motivational speaker. His squatty, five-foot-eight frame was mesmerizing to watch, and fifteen minutes in to any sermon, you started thinking he was taller and thinner. Any sense of timing or word impact I ever developed as a songwriter can be traced directly back to watching my father move souls with the power of words. He would make points, tell stories, offer perfectly crafted arguments, and then call for a decision and commitment from those in the audience who were undecided and uncommitted. When needed, the family Bible story would be summoned and slung into the mix of spirit and humor. I played my part to perfection, half-ashamed, half-cavalier grin on my face and nodding and shrugging at the right times to increase the effect and heighten the laughter. As my dad would recount the genteel story of my toddler epiphany, the old people would ooh and ah, and the young girls would giggle and stare at me with a you-must-have-been-so-cute stare. I admit it; I loved that story. It showed my rebellious nature and unyielding will.

It begins with me placing my tiny hand on the open family Bible perched at the center of our coffee table. According to Dad, I scrunched a page and decided to tear it out. Dad quickly came over, swatted my hand, and said, "No, no, Regie, no, no." His humorous account of the event details me looking him squarely in the eye, pushing out my lower lip, and slowly and deliberately placing my reddened, recently stung hand back on the page while a silent tear rolled down my defiant face. He repeated the chastisement. Swat. "No, no, Regie, no, no." I cried more and took longer to recover but then stared at him again and jutted my hand back to its proper place on the crumpled page. This scene was apparently repeated many, many times. My anger and resolve grew with every cycle of discipline. I was now attempting to tear the page as a matter of principle and not just fun. After all, I found the page. I worked to scrunch it; it belonged to me. The page rip was supposed to happen. I was going to make it happen! It was my destiny to tear that page. Why was my father beating me down and not allowing something perfect and beautiful to happen? There was no fairness to be found here. I was clearly being abused. My reaction would be further defiance and war with the man keeping me from sheer happiness. This had to happen because I wanted it to, and therefore it was supposed to. So I pressed on. In the end, however, an hour of back and forth with the house dictator ended in my defeat. I relinquished control of the beloved, family heirloom to the evil monster keeping me from the joys of destruction. Soon I was not only compliant with the rule of no tearing pages out of the Bible on the coffee table, but the kicker to the story was when a house guest would sit at the couch and try to pick up and read the Bible, I would run over and yell, "No, no, no, no!" The story was a crowd-pleaser of the first order. Often, applause would follow the perfectly timed delivery of the "no, no" hook. It was truly a thing of beauty.

As the story showed, I was not even interested in surrender at the age of two. That attitude continued throughout my life. I was raised in a family of strong people and personalities, individualists, self-starters. I was also a hopeless dreamer. I believed then (as I still do) that dreams can come true. I believed that a posture of defiance and aggressiveness protected those dreams. The man who so masterfully told my two-year-old defiance story had himself been a child prodigy musician. He'd been all over the world by the time he was fourteen and had been on stage with some of the greatest names in gospel music by the time he was fifteen. The year I was born, he was offered a job with Elvis Presley that would've almost certainly catapulted him into stardom but destroyed his personal life. He chose family over career, declined the offer, and then spent the remainder of his life raising my brother and me in church rather than exposing us to the dark world of entertainment. I had vowed not to make that mistake. I made it clear to my wife the night before we got married that I would never give up my dream and that it would behoove her never to ask me to do so. I would sacrifice anything for the dream, but I would never sacrifice the dream itself. The notion of surrender was not a comfortable one for me. In my mind, dreams could be achieved only if you never surrendered. That's what I believed. So it was a difficult and tedious process to dig into the details of surrendering in this song with the iconic title. I will admit that David wrote most of the verse lyrics. He seemed to have a grasp

27

on what it meant to lay it all down at the altar and give your life away. I wanted no part of that.

Every line was talked about and scrutinized. There were at least three more writing sessions of slowly, meticulously combing through the rhymes and reasons. The opening line, "I have wrestled in the darkness of this lonely, pilgrim land," is something I had actually never done. I hadn't wrestled with surrender because I had absolutely no intention of doing it. The "strong and mighty fortresses that I alone command" wouldn't be built in my life for years to come, but ironically, this song would be one of the foundation blocks of those fortresses; its words would later be the wrecking ball.

Just before Christmas 1992, David Moffitt and I sat in an unused office at the publishing company and finally agreed that our five-minute monstrosity was finished. We had painstakingly constructed melody and lyric. We knew it was something; we had no idea what. We went on Christmas break and scheduled a demo session for the first of the next year. What followed was the stuff of dreams.

STARLIGHT

Nashville, Tennessee, in the springtime is one of the most glorious places on our fair planet earth. It is clean and well kept. The bite of bitter winds transform into a gentle expectation slightly brushing through the reborn maples and oaks, and they dance and whisper in their own shadow light. The sudden zephyrs, the rise and fall of every new breeze, are like a deep cleansing breath for all creation. The sapphire skies are warm and cloudless. Antique facades of the Civil War border town get drenched and drowned in newborn sunlight and gleam like the day of their christening. The ancient, brownish-gray, stone slave walls line sidewalks, and in the streets, fresh-faced, taut Vanderbilt and Belmont students, donning running shorts and shoes, gallop through the downtown landscape like new foals in green pastures. The city awakens and stretches from its damp, gray winter and is alive. Nashville is a city built on dreams, and those dreams seem to pulse stronger in the spring. Anticipation hangs in the crisp, Southern air, and it feels like a second chance. On a bright, spring day in Nashville, anything and everything seems possible.

It was on such a day in 1993 that Shawn McSpadden and I found ourselves running at the Vanderbilt University track. We were killing two birds with one stone: getting our daily run in and composing our takeover of the music world. "I Surrender All" had been demoed and was raising a ruckus around the office. I was getting calls daily from other writers and producers telling me how huge that song was going to be. I didn't know what to make of it. I knew the song was well crafted, I knew it was compelling, but I wasn't feeling what everyone else was feeling. Still, Shawn would go on and on about the song. His encouraging and positive nature was a perfect nest for songwriters. As we rounded lap after lap, trying to run off the previous night's excesses of food or alcohol, he told me something I will never forget in breathless, broken words. "This song...is...going to be...your...first...number one. I...also believe it's...it's...probably a...career song for some artist."

"Seriously?" I replied.

"Oh...yeah, man...I'm telling you...this thing...is... huge!" We always referred to Shawn as the man with a heart of gold and tongue of silver. He could sculpt the truth. He certainly knew how to make a creative mess feel like a superhero, and sometimes that required taking certain liberties. But Shawn never played fast and loose with those kinds of predictions. Number one songs are serious business in the world of music publishing. They are the fountainhead from which all revenues flow. They are also as hard to come by as hen's teeth. So no song publisher worth his or her salt ever predicts straight up to a writer that a song that hasn't been recorded yet is without a doubt going to be a number one song. They might say it's a "beast" or a "monster" or any of those cool, music business metaphors we have developed over time for hit songs, but an actual chart position prediction is a no-no. I think the prevailing publisher rationale is to never give someone who's on the verge of killing himself every day too much false hope. It's just not good business.

Why this song? I wondered. *Of all the really cool, hip stuff I've written, why this big, sloppy ballad with all these words about this subject that bothers me so? Why is this resonating with so many people but not with me?* The truth is I was not in a place of surrender, nor did I want to be. That two-year-old boy was still putting his hand on the Bible and grabbing pages. He was determined to rip every last one of them out by the time he was done this time. Still, the oncoming success the song promised outweighed my disconnect with its ominous theme. If this were to be my breakout single, so be it. If it made others want to surrender everything to God's will, so be it. If it helped facilitate a change in someone's life, good for them. I didn't have to sing those words; I only helped pen them. It was craft. I was working for someone else. Some other artist could sing those words with conviction and honesty. I certainly didn't have to do it and wasn't planning to. I was fulfilling my obligations as a staff writer and turning in another viable song for the marketplace, nothing more. We turn in songs all the time that we don't wholeheartedly agree with. We write songs about love gone bad when we're in a stable relationship. We write songs about being in love when we're not. We write about heartbreak when we're happy and happiness when we're heartbroken. That's what we do. We're songwriters. We melt down our experiences and observations and pour them into three-minute pieces of theater for the mind. We wrestle our demons and call on our angels and come out on the other side with a message for everyone else. This just happened to be a song about surrender. So what? It wasn't for me. It wasn't about me. I just happened to be the guy in the room when it was written. I would not be painted into some corner where I had to give up my dreams because some preacher told me to or because some song beckoned. I was me, and that song was that song. We didn't have to like each other; we just had to get along in public and ride with each other to the bank. That was the arrangement we struck.

There were several artists interested in cutting "I Surrender All," but the one who seemed born to sing it was a young Federal Express employee who had signed a management deal with McSpadden Smith management company six months before I'd signed with their publishing company. His name was Walter Clayton Crossnoe, better known as Clay Crosse. Distinctive and soaring, he had the kind of vocal cords record labels are built on. Young and slender with matinee-idol looks and almost cartoonishly perfect, wavy, blonde hair, he was the dictionary definition of the total package. When he walked in the room, you knew a star had just entered. He was that vehicle every songwriter hopes he can attach himself to and place his work in. As he was recording his debut project in the summer and fall of '93, we could feel the excitement building around the office. Everything was pointing to a huge success on the horizon. The label was excited, people were talking, and there was a buzz around town about this guy and the new record he was making. You could feel the rumble of an oncoming train in the distance. It was cool. The centerpiece of this soon-to-be released project was the song David Moffitt and I had so fastidiously assembled almost a year earlier. All signs were indicating it was to be the first single. Those things are never certain until they are, but it felt like it was going to happen, and it gave me a rush. All those years of playing for hours on end—sweaty and exhausted—in long, Pentecostal altar services, all those miles in busses and vans and motor homes to all those tiny church buildings and gymnasiums and tents where I felt like a trained monkey doing flips for peanuts in front of people who didn't appreciate what they were seeing, all those songs I learned and had burned in to my brain, all those hours of practice and learning chords and melodies and harmonies, all those broken-down souls who came to our crusades to find something, anything, and if nothing else, got to watch two little boys (my brother Leny and I), barely big enough to hold their instruments, play and sing like grown-ups—it was all about to melt away. It was all about to be over. I could feel the winds of achievement gently guiding me into what I thought was my rightful place in the sun. Pip was about to become a gentleman. The benefactor would be a song about something with which I didn't agree, but it would be the benefactor nonetheless. I could feel it: my life was about to change.

I got the call every songwriter longs for in the late fall of '93. "I Surrender All" would be Clay's first single released in January of '94. I just had to make it through one more Christmas break. One last hungry year would give way to the success I'd always dreamed of. I could hold out until then. This was going to change the trajectory of my career; I knew it. In January of 1994, "I Surrender All" went out as a single on Christian radio. It was embraced immediately. As Shawn had so accurately predicted a year earlier, it was a monster and did all the things songwriters wish on stars for their songs to do. It climbed up the charts steadily and slowly, never losing momentum. It was critically acclaimed and hailed as triumph for Clay and his burgeoning career. It became a phenomenon and then a stylish video. Then in March of 1994, it became my first number one song as a songwriter and successfully launched Clay Crosse into Christian music super stardom. It was nominated for two Dove awards, including song of the year, and ended up at number three on the year-end radio chart countdown for all songs released in 1994. By all accounts, a song about being willing to give up everything had helped me and everyone else associated with it acquire. "I Surrender All" had ensured that none of us—me, Clay, McSpadden Smith, Clay's label, none of us—would have to really surrender anything for a while. That was fine by me.

Even with a hit song on your resume, professional songwriting is tough business. Your first few years are empty bank accounts, small apartments, old, used cars, and more than one night a week of macaroni and cheese. Sometimes those few years stretch into many years. But if you keep your nose to the grindstone, shoulder to the wheel, play your cards right, and every other cliché ever uttered by the mouth of man, you can turn a random success into a hot streak. I had read the books on songwriters and songwriting, starting from the beginning of the professional trade. I knew the biographies of Irving Berlin, Cole Porter, George Gershwin, Leiber and Stoller, and the rest. Almost everyone in my circle of friends was a songwriter, musician, publisher, or artist. I talked about the music business all day and all night. I knew about momentum and the window of a career. I was intimately acquainted with the possibility of being a one-hit wonder. You could see those guys around town—graying hair and expanding belly, sitting at a bar nursing their medication. "He wrote that big hit such and such for so and so. Never had another cut. I think he paints houses now. Lost all his money in the divorce. Man, he was as hot as it gets for about two years." I was determined to parlay the success of "I Surrender All" into the success of Regie Hamm, the writer. I would not become that guy. I knew that I sucked as a painter and had no college education; my options were limited. I wanted to be a great songwriter, but in order to ultimately achieve that goal, I would have to become a successful songwriter. I had to make this work, so I became a wild man.

I jeopardized my marriage, long-time friendships, and family relationships to be everywhere all the time and be on every record being made in Christian music. I wasn't in love with

Christian music. In fact, I couldn't stand to listen to most of it and found myself drifting further and further from its message. I really wanted to be in pop music; I had a rock star heart and a troubadour soul, but Christian music was where my success had happened, and I knew the Christian world all too well. I was raised with its language and archetypes. I was a believer in and follower of Jesus (I thought) even though I didn't necessarily want to write songs about him all day. Still, I was having success in that part of the music world for that moment, so I took advantage of it. I wrote and wrote and wrote. I joined bands. I started producing records for other artists. Every waking minute of every hour of every day, I was somewhere making music. I was either in the studio or the writers' room or on stage or in a rehearsal or in a label meeting. This was not going to slip away from me. Pip had been at the mercy of a benefactor. His time as a gentleman could've ended at any moment. My success would be self-made and rock solid. I pulled myself up from the bottom to the top, and I wasn't going to lose the grip on my newfound station in life. In 1995, I worked on every holiday of that year, and virtually every other day in between them. I was in the studio on Halloween, Thanksgiving, Christmas Eve, Christmas Day, and New Year's Eve and was on the phone planning the next move on New Year's Day 1996. I was getting songs recorded left and right and singles slated for release. I could see the mountaintop and was ready for the climb.

YOLANDA'S FINE

As a very young man, I had fallen in love with her Latin features—dark, smiling eyes, chestnut hair, skin an exotic blend of mocha and alabaster, statuesque and striking, curvaceous and sultry. She was the girl everyone was afraid to ask out. At five ten, she could look me squarely in the eye, a detail that wouldn't always be pleasant in later years, but that certainly kept us equal. We were both raised in much the same way. Her father was a minister, as was mine. He ministered primarily in the Mexican American community of California and other parts of the Southwest and was bilingual. She was a California native, Los Angeleno, fully informed by the newest trends of the West Coast, yet steeped in the traditions of her Mexican American family, upbringing, and heritage. This made her charm warmly genteel yet more stylish than any woman I'd ever been around. She was, and still is, a gorgeous contradiction, a beautiful mystery.

On our first date, I knew she was the woman I would spend the rest of my life with. She was hilarious yet intelligent and informed. The thing I remember loving the most about her was her ability not to take herself seriously. To a young, brooding, self-indulgent songwriter filled with tragic poetry, she was a breath of fresh air. She was instantly a light in the dark world I had created for myself. I saw it in our first conversation. I knew she was my future in our first kiss. I somehow believed she could save my life. She made me laugh uncontrollably, and we shared the same sarcastic sense of the absurd. She could roll her eyes with the best of them, and her patented "Oh please" spoke volumes. She was a beautiful, Latin, sexy, optimistic skeptic dream girl.

We had married in the middle of my poor years. Having gone bankrupt in my early twenties and now both of us penniless and without prospects, we mutually decided that the prudent thing to do was to go into debt for a wedding as soon as possible. Why be miserable separately when you can be miserable together? We planned, paid for, and executed our own wedding in a blinding seven weeks. Because her father had passed away years earlier, there was no family trust or hope chest for her marriage. She had been supporting her family since her father's death. By the time I came along, any savings, or rainy day funds, were long since used up. It had been raining in her life for years now. Little did she know, when she walked down that aisle to take my hand in marriage, the rain would just be beginning. That three-minute trod to the altar cannot possibly prepare you for the struggles ahead. I'm sure if she could go back in time and talk to herself, she would yell, "For the love of God, woman, you're about to marry a songwriter! Have you lost your mind? The odds of this man being a success at this are like a billion to one! Stop the madness and turn around! You can be friends with him and loan him food money from time to time. You're about to get contractually obligated!" No, instead she slowly marched like a lamb to the slaughter, to hundreds of sleepless nights worrying about bills, to going to bed alone for years on end because her "hero poet husband" was working until dawn, to sacrificing all the creature comforts her friends were enjoying—nice house, new clothes, comfortable car (with air conditioning), vacations, and just general pampering—all because her idealistic spouse was chasing a dream.

My bride got to start her storybook marriage living in my grandmother's house for ten months. Then it was onward and upward to the tiny apartment above a house without central heat and air for the next two years. She had driven those beaten-up cars. She had eaten the macaroni and cheese with me. She'd stared at the empty checkbook. She'd been living the life of a starving artist without the satisfaction of knowing she was changing the world with her powerful words and timeless music. She didn't get to be called a genius every day by those around her. She didn't have the benefit of someone constantly telling her how it was all going to be okay. She had simply gritted her teeth and hung on to a man she believed in. For that, I wanted to give her everything. I had never been ambitious about money or material things, but watching my wife make sacrifice after sacrifice for our first two years of marriage drove me to provide more for her than just a good life. I wanted to give all the finery I could possibly muster. I made her a promise that she probably doesn't remember. I told her in our second year of marriage—after she had just been towed to a mechanic's garage—that if she would just stand with me and hang on a little longer, I would buy her a Mercedes one day, and I would promise on my life that she would never be stranded on the side of the road again in a beat-up, old car. She accepted the promise the way most people accept a panhandler's promise to bring back your five-dollar bill after they've filled the tank of the car that was out of gas down the road. She smiled politely and said, "Okay, baby." I could feel the eye roll when she turned her back. I knew she wasn't taking the promise seriously. But it had become my personal mission: repay this woman for taking a chance on me. Once again, surrender was not an option, and success meant everything.

So with a hit song under my belt, I felt like I was on my way. I had no qualms about burning a swath through the music business at any cost. I had a lot to prove to a lot of people. I wanted to show my wife I could do it, that I could make a living in this insane business and give her everything she'd ever dreamed of. I wanted to prove to those hipsters who had made fun of me in my childhood that I was as cool as them, even cooler. I wanted to prove to an old college professor who once told my music theory class "nobody in this class will ever get that far" after being asked a string arranging question that I indeed would get that far. I wanted to prove to the bourgeois Christian music industry that I was a legitimate talent. Most of all, I needed to prove to myself that I wasn't invisible, that I meant something. I've read the Greek myth of Narcissus. He's the guy we named narcissism after. They say he constantly looked at himself not because he needed a reminder of how beautiful he was but because he continually needed to believe he was actually there. I get that. You can become so involved with yourself that you forget everything and everyone around you. You get so obsessed with your own pain that you can't empathize with anyone else's. The laser focus required to achieve great things can bring with it too much self-indulgence. The more you achieve, the farther away from the actual goal you feel because there is no fulfillment in success alone. It's a meal of empty calories. After you've been given the award or you've left the number one party or you've heard the song on the radio, you're hollow. If you're holding to those things to bring your life meaning, you will never get it. There is no real meaning in them. Therefore, the more of it you get, the less meaning you feel. The less meaning you feel, the more success you crave to fill the void. The more success you have, the less it fulfills you. It's a vicious cycle, and while you're in it, you can certainly become the center of all things. I would say in some ways that happened to me. Flawed motivations. Blind ambition. Faith not needed.

HARD ROCK '95

*I*n the haze that was the mid-nineties for me, one moment stands as the sum of the parts. The phone calls were coming. The radio singles were scheduled to release. The money was out there and would be coming in for years. The relationships were being developed and cultivated. The work was dizzying. To this day, there are chart-topping songs in my catalog I can't remember writing. I know I did it. The physical evidence exists, and you can hear my voice on the demo. The publishing paperwork was all done in accordance with the copyright laws of the United States of America and duly registered with the Library of Congress, but I can't remember, for the life of me, how the songs actually came about. In those days, I had my head in ten to twelve songs a week all the time. I was working my brain down to a fine powder, but the results were starting to show. My second single had come out with a new, young female group called Point of Grace. I had no idea what they were about or who their audience was, but long-time friend and co-writer Joel Lindsey and I had targeted a song toward them. In keeping with the rip-off-an-iconic-hymn-title reputation I was developing, we had written a song called "Gather at the River." It was to be their tenth single. The other nine had gone straight to number one. They were about to be in the Guinness Book of World Records. We were about to help them get there.

While the song was climbing the charts, Joel and I took Shawn McSpadden to Las Vegas for his bachelor party weekend. I had begun to earn enough money to take flights and days off and Vegas vacations and things I never dreamed I'd be able to pay for with song money, but there I was. We were staying at the newly built Hard Rock Cafe Hotel and Casino. It was my first time in Vegas, and I was ready for the glitz and excess. I had been holed up in tiny rooms without sunlight for three solid years. I had been working odd jobs to keep the lights on. I had been doing everything under the sun but vacationing and enjoying myself for longer than I could remember. I was now coming off a number one hit and on the verge of a second one. As our plane was flying over middle America to its decadent destination, the song "Gather at the River" was number three on the CCM (contemporary Christian music, an acronym *everyone* in CCM hates, by the way) charts, and we were all anxious to see if it would rise to the coveted number one spot. I coined an arrogant phrase in those years. "Boys," I would say in a room full of writers, "there are only two chart positions: number one and everything else!" I'll be honest; I wanted that song on top of the charts. An hour before landing, Shawn, Joel, and I procured three tiny bottles of vodka. We toasted our impending success and Shawn's impending nuptials. I walked down the jet bridge into my very first, but certainly not last, Las Vegas experience buzzed and euphoric; it felt like victory.

Three young men in Vegas for a bachelor party can be a dangerous thing. Our three days there proved to be relatively tame. I learned to play blackjack and lose money quickly. Joel won a few hundred bucks on the slots and kept us all fed for the weekend. We generally walked around hotels and took the place in. Even in sin city, though, we were focused. The conversation at every meal would eventually turn back to planning the next move—the next record, the next cut, the next single, the next artist we could work with. The word *one-dimensional* comes to mind. On the third and last day there, we were all sunning ourselves at a private cabana beside the Hard Rock pool. I was eating a bowl of fruit and wondering if my song was doing well. Shawn decided to go call the office and see if the news was good. He emerged twenty minutes later with a huge grin on his face. Joel and I knew immediately the news was indeed good. I sat by the pool at the Hard Rock Cafe, ate fruit, and basked in the success of another number one song. That was the last time I remember where I was when I learned I had a number one record. They would come so fast for the next few years that I would not have time to enjoy them. That moment in Vegas summed it up: success, reward, lying by the pool, and getting the news you're on top. It was awkward, however, because the celebration of that moment had nothing to do with giving thanks to the merciful Father for his allowing such a bounty to be bestowed on me. It had nothing to do with Jesus or his sacrifice. It wasn't sacred. It was crass and drowning in the trappings of hedonism in the Vegas sun. In a way, it was a microcosm of that whole period of my life—spiritual words, material actions, detachment from the news I was proclaiming, being merely a scribe and not a true messenger. I was caught somewhere in the middle of the eternal and the earthly, plying my trade in the realm of the worshipful, yet longing for big time rock and roll. This wasn't big time rock and roll, but it was as close as a church mouse from nowhere had ever gotten. In my mind there was no surrender in sight.

THE BLUR

*T*he professional rocket ship I was on was steady and unwavering. By the end of the nineties, I was having a number one song every six months...literally. That isn't an exaggeration or estimate. Every six months, from 1994 to 2000, I was at the top of the CCM charts as either a writer or producer. One month, I had five songs in the top twenty at the same time. For those keeping score at home, that's 25 percent of all the chart positions. In five short years, my wife and I had traded the quaint, bohemian, upstairs apartment in the city for a sprawling five acres in Franklin, Tennessee, the suburb of choice for those who had made it in the Christian music industry. Our two-story, colonial home was one of only four in a stately cul-de-sac that was wooded and pristine. I could walk onto my back deck and see nothing but trees, rolling land, and a gentle stream that babbled peacefully at the bottom of the yard. We had purchased the two raw acres next to us, ensuring that we wouldn't have neighbors. After all, I needed privacy for my oh so important work. I would descend the staircase every morning—I use the term *morning* loosely, as I would sleep until at least 11:00 a.m. every day—and survey my beautiful home adorned with hip, yet classic wall art and new furniture. I would glance quickly at the big screen TV, round the corner to the kitchen with state-of-the-art appliances, and then yawn as I stared from my back door at the five guys mowing my lawn. I would then walk through my garage, brush my hand across the white Mercedes I had finally bought my wife and presented to her on a certain Christmas Eve with a giant red bow on the hood, and cross the driveway to the one-thousand-square-foot structure that had been converted into a world-class recording studio, complete with two isolation rooms, a large, inviting control room, and floor-to-ceiling windows with glorious views of the wooded acreage. The tiled, glassed-in atrium entrance held all the gold and platinum records I'd racked up over those five years. It was a nice greeting. My commute to work was all of thirty feet, and I walked every step of it with a certain pride that I had acquired it all through the success of my songwriting. Every time I made that trek through the house, past the cars, to the studio, where the sun would bounce off the gaudy platinum, I felt a twinge of accomplishment. *I did this*, I would think to myself. *I made all this happen with my words and music; this is the Regie Hamm estate, purchased with Regie Hamm songs.* As absolutely arrogant and creepy as that sounds, I thought it more than a few times.

By the time I was regularly taking those early afternoon walks to work, Yolanda had been cultivating a successful career as well. She was one of the top radio promoters for a well-known record label in Nashville. She worked with superstar artists and represented hit songs. She had a hefty expense account and knew all the cool places to eat in New York and LA. Every Thursday or Friday, she would be on a plane to some destination to hobnob with radio programmers and DJs. She was always in limos with country and/or rock stars. She was well versed in martini and wine ordering and could close the deal on a hit record without breaking a nail or a sweat. We had both hit our stride professionally. I was locked in the plush studio making magic; she was jet setting with the rich and famous, moving and shaking. The years of struggle had paid off. The macaroni and cheese had tuned to brie and filet. We drank champagne on Tuesdays for no reason. We flew to New York just to shop. We went to Vegas at least four times a year. We went to Europe, the Caymans, St. John, wherever we wanted to go. We were fully participating in the party that was nineties, and in our small circle, we had emerged as a power couple of sorts, complete with all the perks.

In the midst of the blur of success, I became increasingly artistically restless. Doing something successfully means having to do it over and over again. I had been so focused on succeeding as a songwriter in the Christian music industry, I forgot to ask what would happen if I actually *was* successful at it. It was becoming increasingly clear to me that this wasn't where I wanted to be. I felt that I had something bigger to say and wanted to say it a certain way with my own language, my own melodic inflection, my own point of view. I always felt that I was seen with a certain amount of contempt in the Christian community as well. Maybe I was a little too carnal in my lifestyle. Maybe I didn't take myself as musically serious as many CCMers seem to like to take themselves; I could often feel them looking down over their proverbial glasses at me. I really hate pretentiousness. Quite frankly, I finally got to the place where I would get physically ill at being asked to write another knockoff of the latest pop hit. I came to see Christian music as artless and utilitarian. A place anything too far outside the lines would not be welcome. I was outside the lines. Being wildly successful in that world just didn't mean much anymore. I craved a different kind of success now—artistic validation. So I began writing songs in my spare time that I actually hoped would not get recorded. I gave myself permission to venture into any musical or lyrical territory that struck my fancy. I didn't care about radio singles or hits or 3:17, which is supposed to be the perfect length for a radio song, or commerciality or stylistic coherence or any of the things that make you successful in the music business. I just wanted to paint with my own colors. So I did. I started living a musical double life. I would write and produce contemporary Christian music by day for money. By night, I would pack up my keyboard and play my new originals in clubs all over Nashville for art. I can't even count the times I would end a CCM recording session, go in the house to change clothes, load my keyboard in the Mercedes, and drive into town to play a bar or a writer's night. Never once did I ever sing one of my number one records at a club. I always sang the artist material. To this day, people will come up to me in clubs after a show and ask, "Are you the same Regie Hamm who wrote 'Saving the World' or 'The Glory'?" Some have referred to me as a musical Jekyll and Hyde. In some ways, they may be right. Evolving from someone who just wants to succeed into someone who wants to make art is uncomfortable, especially if you are accustomed to a certain lifestyle. That transition would plunge me into very strange and dangerous waters but would ultimately take me to the places I had to go.

AMERICAN DREAMS

By the year 2000, I had compiled enough original material to make what I thought might be a pretty cool record. So one day I looked at my checkbook balance, picked up the phone, and called five musicians on the Nashville A-list. I booked a four-day recording session that would change my life. David Cleveland, Matt Pierson, Gary Burnette, Dan Needham, and Jeff Roach showed up at Darkhorse studios that summer to begin recording what would become the *American Dreams* record. From the first downbeat of the first song, I knew this was what I had been missing. The shackles were off. The road was wide open. This was not just fun; it was what I was born to do. Those guys playing those songs made the world right for me. I had worked with them many times on many different records. We were all great friends. We'd made hits together. We knew the inside jokes and studio shorthand. We had all done this a thousand times before, but this time it was different for me. I was coming alive. The piano room at the small Darkhorse studio had a large window overlooking a horse pasture. With every take of every song, I would sit, play, and watch the horses graze. It was almost as if I'd never seen anything like that before. I felt reborn with every track punch. Scales were falling off my eyes, and things were brighter and more brilliant with every overdub. I told someone this after making that record, and it still holds true today. I felt more like myself during the recording of *American Dreams* than I ever had in my life to that point. By the time the four-day tracking session had ended, I'd spent eighteen thousand dollars out of my own pocket and jumpstarted a new career. There was no going back. Pip was now not only becoming a gentleman but an artist. The days of writing and producing happy Christian songs for happy Christian people had been getting harder and harder to stomach. I was now seeing the end of those days. Another climb, another goal, another, well, dream. Could I be a pop artist? Could I leap from this small world of Christian cheerleading into the legitimate world of real songwriting? Could it sell to the masses? No one knew. Not many believed. A few actually told me I was insane, but I was up for the challenge. I was more than ready for another uncharted journey.

While careers were evolving and successes were being celebrated, Yolanda and I were having trouble behind the scenes. We'd been trying to get pregnant for five years or so. It wasn't happening. In 1998, we went through a procedure called in vitro fertilization. We had heated debates over the procedure. I have always been somewhat of a purist when it comes to these matters, believing if you can't make a baby with your spouse, you should adopt a baby who needs a home. Yolanda was wrestling the will of her biological clock and desire to see a little human being that looked like a combination of her and me. I get it, and I was always genuinely heartbroken for her when it didn't happen. I would certainly love to see what her offspring would look and act like. Mine? Not so sure. Still, we were unable to conceive. The weeks and weeks of shots and reproductive manipulation were all for naught. It was devastating. So we did it again. Yolanda took six months to straighten out hormonally, and we started all over. After weeks and weeks of shots and reproductive manipulation, we didn't conceive the second time either. We sat across from a doctor who very cavalierly told us if he couldn't make it happen, it would never happen. I stood up, looked him in the eye, and said, "You're just a doctor; you're not God." In that moment, I didn't know where my children would come from, but I knew they were out there. I knew they would be coming to me one day. I could feel them before I knew them. I was already thinking about their spirit before I saw their faces. Whether or not they came from me was inconsequential. They were mine, and I would know them when I saw them someday. For now, there was music to make and mountains to conquer. In my mind, it was time to stop worrying about such things and get on with the business of forging the next phase of my career.

Pip didn't worry about things like children and fatherhood. He was singularly focused on becoming something beyond himself, to woo the girl. He didn't plan on what might happen if he actually got her. Neither did I. The becoming was my only concern. At the risk of sounding horrible, I was relieved when we didn't conceive. I didn't want or need anything standing in the way of my new endeavor. I knew it would take everything I had to make it work. I knew I'd have to be gone for weeks and weeks at a time, touring, making appearances, etc. I wanted that more than I wanted children. I knew that it might jeopardize my marriage. I was prepared for the consequences of that. Love, home, and family were just run-of-the-mill by-products of normal life to me at that time. I took it all for granted and thought it was just what regular folks did. If I had a family, fine. If I didn't? Fine, as long as I had my precious career and as long as I kept wowing crowds and racking up accolades. When I think about how I took my wife's love for granted, it makes my stomach hurt. When I realize how cavalier I was with this gift of an amazing life, I am ashamed of myself. But I did, and I was.

After our failure to conceive for the second time, we started reading up on adoption. I was halfheartedly involved. We spoke with friends who had adopted; we went to state agency meetings and watched prepared films on state adoption. We researched international adoption as well. We were slowly becoming experts on the subject and had decided to adopt internationally. The laws in the United States are not uniform from state to state, and many laws favor birth families. If you want to know why people go to China or South America to adopt babies, that's why. It's pretty simple really. No one wants to have some phantom, birth grandmother show up at their child's fifth birthday party and decide to suddenly become a part of the family. Adoptive families should have the right to as much of a normal existence as everyone else. They make the effort to bring the children home. They fight the bureaucracy and pay the legal fees and jump through the hoops. At the risk of sounding like a crusader, adoptive families should get more of the benefit of the doubt than they do. It should be a lot easier to adopt in this country than it is. If you want to see little American children get adopted, read up on your own state's laws regarding adoption and lobby to make those laws as adoption friendly as possible.

As focused as I was on my career, I have always been a huge proponent of adoption. I believe it to be sacred. My great-grandfather was left on a doorstep at the turn of the twentieth century. The Hamm family took him in and raised him as their own. For this reason, I have always been proud of the Hamm name, not because of my bloodline but because of the generations that were galvanized and given legitimacy by one family's selfless act a hundred years ago. As crass as I was toward wanting children, I knew that adoption was (and is) God's work. So Yolanda and I applied to the Chinese government to adopt a little girl. We knew it would take eighteen months to two years. I was skeptical if it would happen at all. I pressed on, not thinking too much about it.

With *American Dreams* basically done and people telling me this was my career changer, I rolled the dice in 2001 and did not renew my huge publishing contract with my large CCM publisher. At the time, I was making one of the highest draws—a monthly advance against future royalties—in Christian music. They offered me the same money to stay. I turned them down. You begin believing your own press. After years of number one songs, songwriter of the year awards, and virtually every dream coming true, you believe you can *will* things to happen. You believe you can achieve anything with enough focus if you're willing to make the sacrifices, if you're willing never to surrender. I believed strongly enough to walk away from a six-figure guarantee. I also called my production clients and told them I was taking time off and not to call me for future projects. Everybody in the music business knows you never make that call. One eighteen-month recording cycle is all it takes for the music world to forget about you. They develop other relationships. They find the freshest and hottest and newest talent. You become the guy they talk about at parties, saying things like, "Where does he live now? Is he still in town? Didn't he get into insurance sales or something?" I was not just cocky but fairly delusional and believed my record and new career were my true destiny. I took a flying leap from Christian music in August 2001. My publishing deal was officially over, and I was completely removed from the system by September 1, 2001. Ten days later, the sky fell.

INFIDELS

*S*eptember 11 was certainly a watershed moment in American history. We all remember where we were when it happened. The days and weeks that followed were those of soul searching and coming to terms with ourselves as Americans. For me, it solidified the need to make your dreams happen while you can. You never know when it all will be taken away. As our eyes were opened to what much of the Muslim world thought of our excesses and ideals, I penned the final tune for *American Dreams*, "Infidels." It was acerbic and biting, and it now made the *American Dreams* record more coherent and gave it the distinct point of view it was lacking. I debuted "Infidels" in New York City around ten months after 9/11, and it got a standing ovation. I was hitting my creative stride. I was seeing the music. You can get to a point artistically where you actually see it before you do it. You feel what your work is supposed to be about before it's actually made. When I meet artists who are just flailing around looking for hit songs, I know they haven't broken through as real artists yet. Real artists know who they are and what they're about. They're taking a journey and asking the audience to come along. They're not asking the audience where they should go. They know instinctively how the road must be traveled, and they travel it as a well-worn path they've been down a hundred times. You can see those artists who know the road and can see the art they're making. You also know the ones who are trying to act like they do. I could see it. The years of honing my craft and finding myself as an artist were coming to an apex. The record I had always wanted to make was now complete and turning heads. Everybody I played it for believed it was something special. For years, pigeonholed as a songwriter/producer, no one really saw me as an artist. I had to change that.

Full-faced and middle-aged looking, the years of working in studios and writer rooms that had turned me into an artist also made me appear a little too comfortable without enough credible edge for pop music. All the celebrating successes with my friends had been catching up to me physically. The wine, vodka, cheeseburgers, and daily Mexican food had made me heavy and unhealthy. I was always an avid runner, but my intake was not so good. After being diagnosed with too many kidney stones to count and given drug prescriptions I would need to take for the rest of my life, I decided to take an unorthodox yet natural approach to healing myself. I made an appointment with a doctor in Virginia Beach who several of my friends had gone to see. They had all experienced amazing, healthy results from working with him. His notions of health and nutrition were radical and certainly not mainstream, but I'd seen asthma, gout, liver cancer, diabetes, and heart disease all cured by his actions and direction. Anyone who has ever had a kidney stone knows you'll do anything to never have another one. I was willing to take a chance on this guy. He looked at my and Yolanda's blood work and put us both on stringent cleanses. No solid food for weeks. A total clean out is not as fun as it sounds. Hundreds of vitamin supplements, gallons of organic vegetable juice, and daily servings of disgusting protein shakes felt like punishment for all the sins we had committed against our bodies over the years. It was one of the hardest and most horrible things I've ever done in my life. But we lost weight. We began looking younger. We began feeling better, and after eight weeks without solid food, I emerged as a new person—thin and clean. Yolanda emerged thirteen weeks later (Yes, I said thirteen. She's a superhero.) looking younger than she did when we got married. Something worked. Our blood work was pristine. We were new creatures inside and out. The doctor did give me one ominous warning. He said, "I can get you to the place where your body is not making any more kidney stones, but the ones already there will eventually have to come out. I have no control over that." Sometimes I really hate dramatic foreshadowing.

Our new lifestyle was set before us. In one spring, we gave up alcohol, caffeine, refined sugar, hydrogenated oil, white flour, and red meat. Cleansing your body from the inside can be a spiritual thing and was life changing for us both. We were now those annoying people you see in restaurants ordering this and that with oil and vinegar on the side, hold this and add that, lightly steam this and serve that raw. "Oh, and could you bring me some more such and such but leave out the so and so." Yep, that was us—food Nazis! The man who had held court at the same Mexican restaurant every day at lunch for years and who regularly started the weekend on Wednesday nights at Beethoven's (the local music biz bar) with friends was now working out a couple of times a day and drinking carrot juice voluntarily! I bought into total health, and it turned my life around. Little did I know that it would play a larger part of the grand design I was about to be a part of. I was no longer self-medicating. I saw a bright, new future. The music was done. Now the vehicle was ready, my new and improved self. I had been making the rounds with the *American Dreams* record to get it signed to a label. If you think looks don't matter in the music business, you're kidding yourself. Once the weight was gone, I was offered two Christian record deals in one week. Not interested. I had my eyes set on bigger things. It was time to become a legitimate artist. When I walked back in to Universal Records forty pounds lighter and looking twenty-five, the label head said to my manager, "Now we can sell him." All the pieces were in place. Pip was now a svelte, healthy gentleman.

BABIES

*L*ight and tight and with what I knew was my best musical offering in my hip pocket, I attacked the new goal
with a vengeance. I secured management by May of 2002. Stuart Dill and Norbert Nix of Refugee Management were excited
and hell-bent on getting my project signed and off the ground. I
was playing clubs every chance I got. I spent my own money to
send the *American Dreams* single out to small radio markets. I was
working it full time. Everyone around me seemed to agree that
the impact song on the record, however, was this little novelty
piece I'd written in my early twenties called "Babies." The song
was like crack cocaine for women. Everywhere and every time I
played it, it brought the house down. I did it once in a packed
club in the Village in New York. A guy in the front row with
a big, purple Mohawk, tattooed like a gang member, and with
earrings connected to his nose ring by long chains was openly
crying like a nine-year-old girl before the second verse was over.
I sort of felt bad for him. He'd spent all that time and money to
look menacing, and I'd blown the whole image in a verse and a

half. This song was money, and everybody knew it. Once again, however, I was focused more on the outcome of singing the song than the words of the song itself: "Oh, but lately, I been thinking that it makes more sense to build a house with a picket fence and forget the Mercedes, get some puppy dogs and training wheels and a family Oldsmobile. I can't believe just how good it feels to be dreaming 'bout babies."

I wasn't dreaming about babies. I had no thoughts about babies whatsoever. I certainly wasn't about to "forget the Mercedes." I was still just trying to become something. Babies were inconsequential to me. The sappy imagery of that song was a means to an end. It brought about a desired effect. It made women swoon. It made guys uncomfortable, which made the women focus on me, the guy brave enough to sing those words, even more. I didn't really care about the women swooning; that's not my thing. What I knew was if women swooned, they'd go buy my records. If they bought my records, I'd be successful enough to get to do this again; that was my thing.

Through a serendipitous (and completely random) turn of events, radio superstar Delilah happened to hear a copy of "Babies" the day she finalized the adoption of her son TK. As I understand it, she walked in the door with him and was immediately accosted by her assistant (who had been sent a copy by my manager) who said, "Okay, you've got to hear this!" She listened, listened again, and then decided then and there to play the song that week. I had not even signed my deal with Universal. In fact, it was still in the negotiation process. A song on Delilah's playlist would certainly seal the deal, but that was a pipe dream. No one got played on the Delilah show without a deal in place. She plays household names and superstars. Her show is not about breaking new, unknown acts. It would be a miracle for her to start playing a Regie Hamm record before it was a hit. Little did I know those words I so cavalierly crooned had impacted her life in such a profound way. The randomness of my introduction to Delilah wasn't random at all. God was using my novelty offering to actually change the course of her life. I wouldn't know the full impact of that song on her for years. That small impact would reach across the world and touch the lives of several more African children who would come to live with Delilah and call her "mommy." At that moment, however, it simply felt like a music business miracle. It was far more than that.

Delilah asked for some mix tweaks to the "Babies" single. My long-time friend and co-producer, Kent Hooper, and I made those changes in a matter of hours. She committed to playing the single on a certain night later that week. Unbelievable! Deal not done, no tour, no video, just a guy with a record, and she was compelled enough to spin it on the largest syndicated (music-based) radio show in the country. This *had* to be a sign from God that I was doing the right thing and in his perfect will. It must have been his ultimate plan for me to be an adored and pampered rock star. This was happening too easily. My thoughts at the time were that I had finally broken through. I had finally shed all the stupid music business opinions and record guys' hesitation. I had jettisoned my quaint upbringing to move into the semi-legitimate world of CCM. Now I would jettison that world for legitimate success and would never look back. I had purified my body. I had made my record with absolute integrity. I had been through the fire of artistry and now was about to be rewarded. It made logical sense to me. This was supposed to happen. It was destiny. It was the moment I had been born to embrace. I had sculpted myself into the total package. I was ready to speak to the world through my music, and the world was ready to listen.

Delilah did, in fact, spin my song without my deal being done, without a tour on the books, without a video on the music channels. Yolanda and I stood in our kitchen and listened to it coming across our little jam box and grinned at each other. "Babies" was played right behind a Phil Collins tune, and it sounded just like it belonged there. I'd heard my songs on the radio hundreds of times, but I'd never heard my voice. It sounded right at home being transmitted through every middle-class housewife's radio in America. When the song ended, Delilah back sold the song, meaning she said my name and the song again, something that isn't always done in radio these days, and Yolanda and I began dancing around the kitchen. Something impossible had just happened. It was a good night.

Now what? So you get a song played on the radio? It can mean nothing, or it can mean everything. This was starting to mean something. The next few days were a barrage of e-mails from the Delilah people telling us of the incredible response to the song. She would be playing it again; the fans had spoken. With the news of this in hand, Universal Records finally committed to leasing my master of *American Dreams* (without one solitary change) and releasing it nationally. I was being signed as an artist to the largest record label in the world. They had agreed to release my self-produced record without any changes. All thirteen of my solo written songs would be on the record in the exact sequence I put them. This was a spectacular achievement. Even now, on the other side of it, I still know what an accomplishment it was to bring an unknown, self-written and produced project to a major record label and have them sign it as is without any changes. It certainly felt like providence to me. It also felt like invincibility, like destiny, like the foregone conclusion and storybook ending to a fairy-tale career. Songwriter takes risk, risk pays off, and everyone lives happily ever after.

Delilah scheduled a phone interview with me that week. Four days later, I was doing bumpers for her show over the phone. The label was setting the song up for national release as a single. The lawyers were tying up loose ends on the deal. This was happening. She was on the verge of adding the song to her playlist. That would be a huge thing. A couple of plays were one thing; being added to the playlist was a solidification. It meant you're here to stay. It was more than any record label could hope for out of the box. I was finding myself in the business of doing more than you can hope for. *American Dreams* coming true.

We made arrangements to fly to Seattle after the first of the year in 2003 and do a small radio tour of a few stations in that area, as well as an in studio visit with Delilah herself. The label was hoping we'd get her to officially add the single. She'd been playing it through the fall of 2002, and in October of that year (just before the Christmas break), it was her most requested song of the month. She would forward e-mails from listeners who wanted to find the record. "Who is this guy and where can I get more music from him?" was the ever-present question in those e-mails. One trip to Seattle and we'd be one step closer to answering that question for the general public. I can't even remember Christmas of 2002. All I remember is sitting in a lawyer's office, signing the record deal, and getting a large advance check. I honestly don't remember anything after that until I was walking through the airport to fly to Seattle in January of 2003.

FLYING

While I was watching my new career lift off the ground, a newborn baby was struggling to survive in a rural village of southern China. I didn't know her. I wasn't thinking about her. I was singing songs and making a name for myself. She was strapped in a crib, wearing handed-down clothes that were too small, getting six bottles a day (I've always hoped), and simply surviving. She was born on July 30, 2002, in the middle of my scheming and strategizing to become a pop star, and was placed on the doorstep of the local orphanage that very day. Chinese law prohibits more than two female children per household. If you have a boy first, you've met your quota, and you're not to have any more children. If you have a girl, you can try once more for a boy. Obviously, boys are placed at a higher premium, and girls are, well, seen as slightly more inconvenient, let's say. Couples producing more than their share of children are taxed the equivalent of a year's salary (around 2,600 American dollars). If you can't pay the fine (and no one can), you could be placed in prison. Bearing children out of wedlock is also a punishable offense. The barbaric laws of a communist regime have forced many Chinese mothers into the marketplaces and orphanages of those villages with baskets carrying wrapped, newborn children, mostly little girls. They tearfully leave those baskets in public areas to be found by orphanage workers. They know that more likely than not, Americans will be coming to adopt those children. This is not abandonment; it's love in its rawest and rarest form. As a result, China has a staggering surplus of little girls in orphanages all over that country. There are literally millions of them waiting for someone to come get them. This little girl was one of the millions, the homeless residue of Mao's utopian vision. She was hanging on by less of a thread than anyone could've known and waiting to change my life.

The eight-hour, cross-country flight was exhausting. But as we touched down in Seattle, I immediately put on my game face. I was ready for this. It was the first step in the grand unveiling. Stuart, my manager, was sitting next to me.

"Time to knock it out of the park, dude," he said with a smile.

"I brought my bat," I said, smiling back. I've always loved pithy retorts. Riding in the back of the rented SUV to the hotel, I drummed my fingers nervously on the window. I felt like a rock star already. We checked into the five-star hotel and went to our rooms. My lovely, tailored suite was already turned down with a chocolate on the pillow. A gift basket and note awaited me. Someone had handwritten the obligatory: "We're so happy to have you in Seattle and can't wait for the show." I popped open the raw almonds and ate a handful. I thought, *Feels like home here. I'm finally being treated the way I deserve to be.* While a little Chinese girl was freezing and squirming in her crib in a room full of other screaming orphans while fussy caregivers were yelling over the baby noise and dealing with everything from bed linens to baby poop, I was casually flipping through channels. A little Chinese girl was getting her bottle of cheap formula; I was reading the room service menu. She was being swaddled in makeshift rags; I was hanging up my rock star clothes and deciding on my look for the following day.

After a six o'clock wake-up call, I lay there in the darkness, thinking about the day's itinerary. This day could change my life forever. After around fifteen minutes of pondering, stretching, and yawning, I bolted up and quickly dressed into my workout clothes. The hotel gym was across the street. I ran across the dark, damp street, through the smoke that was belching from the manhole covers. By six thirty, I was in the torture chamber—weights and a three-mile run. Today, I could lift more; I could run faster. My adrenaline was carrying me to new plateaus. My final five minutes on the treadmill were like a scene from a Rocky movie. I kept raising the rate of speed until I was in a full sprint. I jumped off the treadmill and ran back to the hotel without stopping or slowing down. This was my day. Time to be what I was born to be. I felt my power. I dressed and met both my managers in the lobby of the hotel right on time, fresh and ready. The first item on the agenda was a photo shoot with Delilah at her home—cake.

I walked in to Delilah's surprisingly average, yet incredibly warm, home to find no less than three nannies on hand and children in every corner of the place. As a friend once told me, "Delilah's house must smell like mother's milk." It did. I smiled when I entered the child-laden abode. Delilah came out, we met, and I met the children. There were so many, I could not remember them all if a gun were put to my head. Finally we started shooting pictures. Delilah kept talking to me about my pending adoption. I was answering in cautious phrases. I had no idea when or if China would call. I wasn't really thinking about it all that much. I was building a career here. She wouldn't let it go;

she asked about details between photo setups. I politely gave as much information as I had, but I wasn't concerned about Chinese babies at the moment. I was concerned about the song; tell me again how much you like it. It's really cool, isn't it? Your audience is loving it, aren't they? She kept talking about family, and it was annoying. I was there to promote a single; she was interested in my heart. This superstar voice that I heard on the radio every night kept talking to me about things I wasn't prepared to talk about—the heart of the matter, the reasons for my song, the soul of it all. I hadn't found that yet.

I was just a driven songwriter with a misguided gift, a crooked little diamond who'd almost pulled himself out of the rough. Didn't she know I had financed the project with my own money? Didn't she know how many number one songs I'd written? Hadn't she heard all those cool lyrics on that record? How could she have missed just how clever I was? Didn't she realize I had done all this against the odds? Surely that was enough. No, Delilah was interested in family and love and adoption and children in need, spiritual things completely unrelated to the fleeting and fickle entertainment business. She had several adopted children and her producer, Jane Bulman, also had an adopted child. They were about love and giving of yourself to those who need you. They practiced absolutely everything they preached. I had gone to Seattle to find radio success and a bigger audience. What I found were unexpected friends and angels who were trying to gently guide me down a better path. It would take years to fully realize that. I didn't know quite how to feel. All I could do was look as pretty as possible and sing and play my piano real good. It had worked my whole life. Surely it would work now.

The two days in Seattle were packed with radio interviews, performances, and telling the story of the "Babies" song over and over and over again. It's actually a pretty good story. I did literally dream about babies one night. After watching an uncommon number of fathers in a mall, holding purses for their wives and tending to small children, I went back to the hotel I was staying in and dreamt about babies all night. I woke up and sang the refrain in the shower that morning. "I've been dreaming 'bout babies"—crowd-pleaser every time. I performed in the lobby of one of the radio stations there in Seattle; I had just finished the song and was working the crowd, smiling at all the girls in the room, and generally laying on as much charm as I could muster. The program director asked me a couple of questions after the song. He then said something I'll never forget. He looked at me and said in a loud voice for the whole room to hear, "Young man, if you were a stock, I would sell all my other stocks and invest in you alone. You're going to be a superstar like we've never seen in this business!" That statement was followed by laughter and then spontaneous applause. That was the program director. I knew in that moment that I had the add at that station but, more importantly, I knew this was a sign of things to come. Program directors always play it close to the vest and never tip their hand. This one was openly fawning over me in front of his station. I winked at my managers; they smiled back. We knew this was not just good but spectacular. And so it went; knock it out of the park, I did. Back in Nashville, the head of the New York office of radio promotions happened to run into us in the airport. He was working my single and passing through.

"Hey, you're Regie Hamm?" he yelled.

"Yes, sir. In the flesh," I said with a coy smile.

"Man, everybody at Universal has Regie Hamm fever right now. You're happening, bro! Got to catch my flight. Get ready for the tidal wave!"

Game on.

My wife had done his job. I needed to hear good things from

this guy. I knew this was the best news possible. Every station we had visited in Seattle had added the record the following week. The reviews of the performances were coming in, and all were off-the-charts great. Regie Hamm had conquered the soft rock market in that part of the country. Finally, Delilah sent word that she was adding the song to her playlist as well. Everything that could've gone right did. With all of those adds coming in, "Babies" was burning through the adult contemporary charts with a fever. It entered in the high forties and then soared quickly into the top twenty. I had seen this happen years earlier with my friend Bob Carlisle. His song "Butterfly Kisses" had taken the world by storm in much the same way. I'd been an observer of that rocket ride and knew all too well of the rewards. Bob and I had ridden in limos together. We'd blown obscene amounts of money on dinners just because we could. I had been to Bob's mansion in Vegas many times. We'd sat beside his pool and joked about the salad days. Having a phenomenal hit is filled with perks you can't believe. You don't stand in lines (and I *hate* standing in lines). You get invited to the cool parties. You are catered to at every turn. Someone is always there to make you as comfortable as possible. This was all about to happen for me. It wasn't a dream anymore; the sheer realities of the charts were proving it.

Not only were the charts edifying my work, but the critics started doing it as well. I've always had a love-hate relationship with critics. You can inadvertently say the wrong thing in an interview and suddenly get a bad review from that interviewer in that interviewer's publication; it has happened to me on more than one occasion. This time, however, the angels were on my side. The reviews that came in were not just good but kind of unbelievable. I was being compared to the likes of Randy Newman and Jimmy Webb. One reviewer called me the "second coming of Elton John." I had several "best record of the year" quotes and even one "maybe the best new record of the millennium" kudo. Okay, maybe I dreamed that one; I can't find it on the Internet anymore. Even for someone as confident as I was, this was too much to hope for and actually quite humbling. For a brief few months, I was lightheaded with success, both critical and commercial. I could literally do no wrong. Everybody loved the new me. I was going to be a star. As the single climbed the charts, every morning was a new and exciting phone call from my manager's office. One call was especially strange but intriguing.

"How would you feel about opening for Cher on the April leg of her farewell tour?"

This was like three farewell tours ago.

"Will her audience get me?" I asked.

"It doesn't matter; you have a hit song. You'll do thirty minutes and then break into that song, and they'll go crazy. That's what hit songs are all about."

I remember that I was lying in bed, not yet up and about that morning. I just smiled a sleepy smile and said, "Book it; I'm in."

"Details to follow" was the last thing I heard about that tour. Those calls were happening almost every day. There was talk of three dates with Willie Nelson, a week with the Dixie Chicks— this was pre-foot-in-mouth Dixie Chicks. There were rumblings of European tours and stints with cool rock bands. The William Morris Agency was my booking agent, and they had access to everyone. As long as my single kept climbing, there was almost no limit to what they could do for me. At one point, I was in a meeting with the actor-musician liaison for that company. She asked if I wanted to get into acting. I was so taken aback by the notion, I just said, "Well, I've never really thought about it, but not really." She was visibly surprised. Who doesn't want to be an actor? Me. I just need a piano and fifteen minutes, and I'll make 'em laugh, cry, feel, think, and everything in between without ever having to go to a 6:00 a.m. call time. That was my attitude.

Yolanda and I had a week of downtime before the touring and radio insanity set in. We decided to go to Vegas to celebrate. Although things were amazing on the career front, we were really starting to drift apart as a couple. I was always off at a meeting or a gig, applying my work ethic to everything. She was taking college courses, learning Spanish, and trying to have some fulfillment in her own life. I could actually start to see this marriage ending, and as cold as it sounds, I was fine with it. What I had wanted my whole life was in the palm of my hand. If it cost me my marriage, that was actually a price I was willing to pay. I think we both thought going to Vegas and having fun like we had once had would rekindle something between us; it didn't. That trip to Vegas was one of the most boring times I've ever had there. I think Yolanda would probably agree. We had nothing to talk about except my pending rock-star status, of course. I was completely preoccupied and certainly not focused on her in any way. She was growing increasingly disinterested with me as well. I can't blame her; I would've hated me by that time. My career was dominating our lives in every way. Our existence was filled with it constantly. Anything not placed in proper balance can stifle love—careers, tragedies, illnesses, hobbies, even churchgoing. I've known seemingly humble pastors who simply *must* talk about their churches at every conversation. I've known recording artists who didn't make it, and they have this need to retrace the steps of their undoing every time you see them. Even people with health challenges who make their particular challenge the focus of their lives are missing out on something. When you become obsessed with something, it becomes your idol. This new career of mine simply took all the air out of the room. I think it was getting harder and harder for Yolanda to breathe.

The time in Vegas couldn't end soon enough. We were in the airport waiting to board the plane, and I decided then and there that I was going to ask Yolanda for a separation on the flight home. We were clearly growing apart, and I was simply not going to slow down in the building of this career. I was aging, and I knew my window for ultimate success would be small. I had to make it happen now; I would not get a second chance at this. Our marriage would probably be a casualty. This happens all the time in the entertainment world. Besides, we had no children, and I had pretty much given up on the Chinese adoption coming through. We needed to be apart, and I needed to be able to focus, tour, and really make this happen. After all, it was my destiny.

As we sat in the airport waiting to board, my adrenaline was rushing. I'd made up my mind to have the talk with Yolanda once we were settled in our seats with four uninterrupted hours to hash it out. I knew there would be tears and awkwardness. Still, I really believed this had to be done. She didn't seem happy with me anymore. I just wanted to be something. In my mind, she was standing in the way of me reaching my truest potential. About ten minutes before we were to enter the homebound aircraft, Yolanda got a call on her cell phone from an unknown number. She answered.

"Yes, this is Yolanda Hamm. Oh my! Really?" Yolanda looked at me in tears.

Did someone die? I thought to myself.

"How old? Eight months. Yes, yes. She's got … and … oh, sweet … of course we're ready … when we get home … we'll … six weeks … okay, thank you … oh, very excited! Thank you! Thank you! Thank you!"

I knew it; we were getting a baby. Yolanda hung up the phone and began spilling the news in excited and tearful tones. I was hyperventilating. This *could not* be happening to me! Not now! Not when I was on the verge of the ultimate breakthrough. Six weeks? In six weeks, when I should be in the thick of radio tours and opening for superstars, I was going to be on a plane to China. Why would God do this to me? Was this some sick joke? This was a cruel twist by a slave master who had tried to keep me down my whole life. I would not surrender. This was his way of making me stop moving forward. He wanted to relegate me to his small congregations and his utilitarian, subpar brand of music without poetry or irony or any of the things I was striving to achieve. This is why all the good music was made by pagans; they would stand in defiance to this crippling turn of events. Bob Dylan wouldn't put his career on hold to go adopt a baby just because his wife needed something in her life. Billy Joel would've divorced his needy wife years ago. I had been a good guy. I had been faithful. All I wanted was my time in the sun. God, as he always had before, was going to let me get close enough to smell it but never taste it. This little Chinese girl was about to wreck my career. *Thanks, God. Thanks a lot. I could've been a shining example to the secular world that Christians can make art as well as anyone else. I just needed time and some luck. You just messed the whole thing up.* These were the thoughts that were racing through my muddled mind. I could feel my face getting red—anger, surprise, confusion, more anger.

Yolanda was visibly displeased with my reaction. She wanted me to jump up and down and be ecstatic. Instead I was pacing and darting my eyes and probably looking like a man trying to escape something.

"I have to go to the bathroom and splash some water on my face; this is too much to take in," I said, trying to seem overly excited and happily stunned; I was neither. I left Yolanda standing in her emotions and went to find the bathroom. The terminal was closing in. I couldn't tell where I was. The airport was a blur of faces and shoes walking to destinations. I searched for signs. *There's a bathroom; duck in there.* I ran in and began splashing water on my face. I couldn't get a handle on the moment. I stared into the sink and then up to the mirror. Suddenly, I realized that a dozen women were frozen and staring back at me. I had walked squarely into the women's restroom.

"Oh my... I am sorry, ladies... I just found out I'm going to be a dad," I said. They smiled, and I backed out of the restroom politely.

"What's wrong with you?" Yolanda demanded.

"I'm just freaking out a little. There's so much to do, so much to think about, not much time, you know, dad stuff."

Yolanda has never been good at concealing her emotions. She was scathingly angry at me. I had completely ruined the news of our pending adoption. I was distant and obviously not as into this as she was. "You really know how to destroy a beautiful moment," she said, choking back tears. "I need you to be happy about this!"

"I am. I am. Just let me process it. This has been a long time coming. I have to work it out in my own way." The flight back to Nashville was cold and uncomfortable. A million thoughts raced through my head. I knew what had to be done in order to be a successful artist. A wife and baby would not survive it, not if I really did it right. I'd been in the music business a long time, and I knew what it would take. Still, I could not back out on the child now, not after knowing she was waiting on us. I was a self-obsessed, but I wasn't a monster. I knew we had to go get this baby. For the next few hours, I organized and arranged in my head how it could work. I wouldn't be home a lot but neither was my dad growing up. I turned out okay... sort of. Maybe this could be done. By the time we landed, I had settled it with myself. I was breathing again. I was making a kind of peace, however uneasy, with this unknown little girl, whoever she was. It was a small surrender.

GOD BLESS THE BABIES
IN CHINA

*S*ix weeks. I had six weeks to figure out how to organize a home life and a career as a rock star. The sad truth is it's almost impossible to do. Yolanda and I talked and schemed and compromised and finally came to an uneasy truce in the battle over career and family. She had been in the music business too. She knew what I would have to do to keep the artist thing afloat, and strictly from a business standpoint, we didn't really have much of a choice. I'd unceremoniously left Christian music—my main source of income—and had no more production clients. I had no publishing deal, and any deal I would've been offered by any secular company would be half of what I needed to survive. I simply had no track record anywhere but Christian music. So now, even from a family practicality standpoint, this had to work. We were about to have another mouth to feed. The dream had collided with cold reality.

It came in the mail not long after we returned from Vegas. We sat on our bed and stared at it for at least five minutes before opening it. Finally, Yolanda said, "I can't take it anymore!" and we ripped open the envelope and gazed at her—our little girl in a five-by-seven picture, completely bald and wearing layers and layers of mismatched clothes. She had a scowl on her face, that beautiful, angelic face. The scowl said, "Dad, what's up? Get over here and get me! I'm uncomfortable, and I'm in freaking China! Get here now!" It was (and still is) the cutest scowl I'd ever seen. The emotions were so hard to put into words (and I make a living with words). Most expecting couples see ultrasound images of a developing fetus, a life not yet exposed to wind and rain, sights, and smells. The imaginations of the parents superimpose what the child might one day look like and what their personalities might be. All of those imaginations and thought processes are informed and colored by the world in which they themselves live. The little girl in this picture already had a personality; it was clear. She was covered in the trappings of a culture I knew very little about, ten thousand miles away. She'd already been held and fed and changed and rocked. After staring at her picture for several days, I started wondering throughout the day what they were doing with my daughter that day. How were they treating her? How was she feeling? Did she get enough to eat today? Motherhood happens instantly; women know and feel instinctively what they're supposed to do. Yolanda was already nesting like a hen. Fatherhood, on the other hand, happens more gradually as the man begins going through the logic of the situation. My paternal instincts were flickering like that florescent light in the basement that tries to come on for several minutes. Once it does, it's on forever. It would be the same with me eventually.

American Dreams was scheduled to release (or drop) on March 18, 2003. Our plane for China left on March 21, 2003. You can't really cut it much closer than that. One thing I knew for sure was that by mid-April, my life would be very different one way or another. We shopped for cribs and pink baby sheets and had showers and got tons of frilly little girl clothes from family members. In a matter of weeks, the room we never went in had been transformed into a sanctuary of stuffed animals, lace-covered blankets, and more clothes, hats, and shoes than would ever be worn by the soon-to-be princess. There was a tug-of-war in my mind over Isabella's adoption and the CD release. I had kind of bought into spoiling a little girl and couldn't wait. On the other hand, I'd *really* bought into hanging out with superstars and becoming one myself. If both could be achieved, it would be a miracle. Put the blinders on, go fetch this little girl, get home, and go to work. That was the focus. In the meantime, a small wrinkle called SARS was enveloping Asia. People were dying. You never think about stuff happening in Asia until you're about to go to Asia. I casually called the CDC to get instructions on how to proceed.

"Under no circumstances should you get on a plane to China right now, sir," was the startling answer that came back over the phone.

"My daughter's over there; I have to go."

"Sir," said the woman with the stern, clinical voice, "I cannot tell you what to do, but I strongly advise you not take this trip."

This wasn't good, but there was no way on earth Yolanda wasn't getting on that plane. She was already a mom. I was trying to make sense of it, but I knew we would be going to China, SARS or no SARS—one CDC recommendation ignored, more to come.

On March 18, we held a release party at a small club in Nashville. I played the entire CD live with a band. The place was filled with friends, family, and people from the booking agency, record label, and management company. The good will was palpable. We had a large picture of Isabella made for me to place in front of the piano at the end of the show when I did "Babies." The name given to Isabella at the orphanage where she had been placed was Xin Meng (pronounced sing moong), which means "new dreams" in Mandarin. The irony of that was never lost on me. I had written a song with the hook "I've been dreaming 'bout babies" that was a hit single climbing the charts. The name of my CD was *American Dreams* and was basically a stroll through the American landscape of dreams—the dreams of the rich, the poor, the immigrants, the entrenched middle class, my own dreams of the past and present, broken and realized, hazy and vivid. The culmination of my work from "I Surrender All" to *American Dreams* had been about my own becoming as an artist and a man. And now, in this listening room, awaiting the launch of this new career, the dream I had made come true, the classic American success story with all the drama and what appeared to be a happy ending, was a picture of a little girl with this haunting name…"New Dreams." As I sang "Babies" in that room, I broke for the first time in my many years of singing it and started crying. Suddenly, as I was singing those words, I knew there was something deeper about to happen to me, something I'd never felt. Why did she have to have *that* name? I had written all I could write about dreams, I thought. I had created a landscape of dream sequences in what I was being told was a masterpiece. Now, God was sending me another ominous message: "You're about to have new dreams."

"What was wrong with these old ones?" I wanted to shout.

I finished the set, smiled as the crowd applauded, and went to dry my eyes and mingle. I walked off the stage and looked back at the picture resting in front of the piano. It was an image that would define the next six years: Isabella in front of my piano, in front of my dream, in front of my identity. I stared at that delicious face and couldn't get a handle on my emotions. But I heard a still, small voice saying over and over again, "New dreams, Regie, new dreams. Not just the kind you've been chasing, new dreams—her very name given to her by some unknown rural orphanage worker ten thousand miles away is new dreams. That is not random."

After a show, you're still high from the hormones released during the playing and hearing of music. It takes me a few minutes to think straight and speak coherently. The first person who accosted me was my booking agent from William Morris. "You lost vocal strength toward the end. Get in shape; you're going to be busy," were the first words out of his mouth. Entertainment is work, period. I've heard stories of even the likes of Springsteen getting ripped by his label for not having good shows in the early days. Too much money rides on it; you have to be on. These guys were about to tell the world how great I was; I knew I had better deliver when I showed up. Still, I had been doing this since I was five years old. I'd been doing it for money since I was ten. I knew how to do a forty-five-minute set in my sleep. This was no big deal; I was just a little out of shape. I'd been buying baby stuff for three weeks. I'd be ready.

"Do you have a nanny lined up yet?" he asked in a terse way.

"We're working on it; this is just all happening so fast."

"Well, get your nanny lined up and get ready to tour. We're talking about possibly putting you on some shows with the Goo Goo Dolls in Europe this summer. You could be gone for weeks. Seriously, get in shape, and get a nanny." Then he gave me the parting smile and half-hug and said the obligatory, "Dude, you rock, and we're incredibly excited about you. You're going to be a superstar. Just get ready to work." He and his staff then left me to wipe the sweat out of my post-show hair and ponder all those heartwarming thoughts. My line of sight was directly on the picture again once he stepped out of the frame. "New dreams" kept coming back to me.

The next day was a haze of packing. Going to Panama City for a weekend is easy to pack for. Going to the other side of the world for three weeks and coming back with another human being is like a preparing for a military operation. I can't even count the trips to Walmart and Target to get stuff made in China to take to China. My head still spins thinking about the numbers of diapers and bottles and formula and bottle warmers and rattlers and onesies and twosies and on and on and on. Yolanda and I took three pairs of cargo pants and ten T-shirts each. We kept it tight and light and decided to wash every few days rather than pack like nineteenth-century debutantes traveling west with steamer trunks full of nonessentials. It was minimalist and sparse. We took our vitamins and food substitutes. We would be the healthy parents with the organic formula and no pharmaceuticals. Live by example. We were going to be a shining light of health and natural approaches to caring for an infant—best-laid plans, as they say. We were packed and ready for my mother and father to drive us to the airport. The next time anybody saw the high-flying, party couple Yolanda and Regie, we'd be sporting a Chinese baby. Good-bye, old life; hello, parenthood.

We had a four-hour flight from Nashville to LA. I don't remember a thing about it. Next there was the one night layover in LA and then new dreams. What did all this mean? It was so very inconvenient to bring a baby into the mix of the rough and tumble world of pop music. Did I just have bad luck? Was there a plan or purpose here? Why was this name, "new dreams," haunting me so? I knew it was God's way of sending me a message, and it pissed me off. I believe God sends you messages in ways he knows you'll get. For some, it's just a feeling. Others claim they actually hear an audible voice. That's never happened to me. God knows that I'm a writer, a storyteller, and artist. I pay attention to things like irony, paradoxes, foreshadowing, conflict, and contrast. He knows I'm constantly looking for the hook. Therefore, he—very annoyingly, I might add—speaks to me in that language. I know he placed David Moffitt in my life to purposely write that blasted song, "I Surrender All." He was sending a message; I knew it even then. Now, he sends this little girl with this name, "new dreams," in to my life at this particular time. I knew it wasn't a random coincidence, and it bothered me greatly. I didn't want new dreams. I wanted *my* dreams to come true. I didn't want to surrender. I wanted to achieve everything I had been working toward on my own terms by my own hand. Once I got on the plane to China, this would all be in motion, and God would, at least partially, have what he wanted. I was disturbed.

That night in LA, Yolanda and I went to see a movie and chill out before the following long day that awaited us. Yolanda's sister lives in LA, so we met with her, went to dinner, and then went to Santa Monica to catch a flick. While waiting for the movie, we ducked into a record store and went to the H bin in the pop/rock section. I rifled through the CDs, and then there it was. *American Dreams* was in the record store in Santa Monica. There was the sticker: "Featuring the smash hit 'Babies.'" There was the bar code. There was my face on the back. This was real. My heart kind of fluttered, and I couldn't contain the smile. Against the odds, I was in the record store in the *pop* section. Three weeks in China and I could get back to business. Yolanda and I left the record store and disappeared into the dark theater; it would be the last time we would sit in a theater together for the next four years.

On the day of the twenty-first, I decided to go for a walk to clear my head before we boarded for China. Putting on my clothes and doing the about-to-be-seen-in-public rituals of hair and teeth and the like, I could hear George W. Bush in the background giving the people of Baghdad a warning to leave. War was imminent. *Great*, I thought. *First SARS, now a freaking war's about to start while my wife and I are in international airspace! Anything else, God?* I walked out the front door of the Embassy Suites hotel dazed and reeling. My mind was traveling in a million different directions. Once I got on this plane, it could all be over. Raising a baby would be tough while trying to break as a pop star. My dad had been gone a lot when I was a kid. I never wanted that for my children. I'd hoped my traveling days would've been over by now, and here they were just beginning. This wouldn't be fair to this little girl. She would be better off without me. Yolanda would be better off without me. I knew I was self-centered. I should just keep walking into downtown LA and disappear. I could just never go back. What if I simply sank into the thirteen-million-person landscape of this city and reemerged as an actor or got in touch with the Universal office in LA? William Morris could book me out here. The story of how I was this close to getting on a plane to China but then backed out at the last minute could be an interesting story on a talk show, couldn't it? No pop music buyer would care if I was married or had kids. It would be a blip on the radar screen on some tabloid Hollywood reporting show. My blood was racing, and my adrenaline was high. With a flushed face and a fluttering heart, I was walking faster, turning corners and staring obsessively at cracks in the sidewalk.

"Keep walking, Reg. This family thing is going to destroy all your dreams. The greats make tough choices. The legends don't surrender or let someone else dictate their life. A legend would be true to himself and keep walking. You can be a legend; you have that level of talent; everyone says so. You're about to throw it all away for some little girl in China who will probably get adopted by the next family in line the next day. Keep walking. Stay right here in LA. Go be a star," said the independent voice with the mean streak. I was running now, and my breathing was difficult.

"Reginald Hamm, get your selfish butt back to that hotel and do the responsible thing. You have people depending on you. Hamm men don't abandon people; we take babies off doorsteps and raise them. Do your duty as a man," said the guilt voice. I could feel myself breaking into tears.

"I don't want new dreams. I don't want new dreams. I want to be successful. I want to finally make it out of the music ghetto I came from. Only a tough choice will get me there. Getting on that plane will make me normal and mediocre. I can be a legend. I have that kind of talent, and that's all that matters. Run, Regie. Get away from that ball and chain that will drag you into slavery. This baby is going to be difficult. There's something to that new dreams thing. It's going to mean something bad for you. Keep running. Leave them. Get free. Don't look back. Dylan, Joel, Elton, Bruce—you can't be those guys without sometimes being an SOB. Keep running."

As the LA traffic buzzed around me, I stopped and looked up. I'd been looking down the whole time. Where was I? I had to get back to the hotel. *I need Yolanda. I need my wife, and I need to meet Isabella*, I thought. *She's a real person, and she's waiting on me.* I turned around and started sprinting back the way I had come. In full gallop now, I looked at my watch. There were only ten minutes until we were supposed to leave for the airport. I ran faster, past burger joints and strip clubs and through "don't walk" signs. Finally, I rounded a corner and ran right into the Embassy Suites portico. There was Yolanda sitting in the car, smiling at me. "You get lost? I was starting to get worried. I've got us packed and ready."

"I thought I was lost there for a minute, but I'm okay now. Let's go get our girl."

In the airport, we did all the usual stuff: checked our bags, hugged my sister-in-law good-bye, and found the gate. I'd begun videotaping the experience and was finding other families who were in our adoption group. Yolanda was in the restroom, and the families were starting to ask me questions (on camera) I couldn't answer.

"What province is your daughter from?" I had been so focused on myself and the record release, I honestly didn't know. My eyes darted, and I said, "You know, I never pronounce it right." One lady reeled off all the provinces from which we would be getting children. "Which one of them?" I suddenly felt like a kid who couldn't work the problem on the chalkboard. My face was flushed with embarrassment. "Um, say the third one again? That sounds right." They were staring blankly at me. One mother was clearly disgusted with my obvious ignorance. Just then, Yolanda showed up. "Honey, what's the name of Isabella's province again. I'm always forgetting how to say it," I said with a nervous smile. Yolanda instantly knew it and rattled it off. I was ashamed of myself. I had never cared enough to learn it. I couldn't pronounce it because I had no idea where she was born. I hadn't been interested enough to pay attention. This was the first time I'd actually listened to Yolanda say the word *Xianji* (pronounced jiang she). Now, for the first time, I realized that this too was real.

Six couples boarded the airliner to Guangzhou, China, all of them carrying no less than ten thousand dollars in concealed cash. We would meet up with twenty other families the following week. We were all going a few days early to take in the sights of Beijing. I mean, how many times do you get to China? We figured we might as well make a trip of it. One thing the Hamms knew how to do was travel well. That would end soon enough. The fourteen-hour flight was calm and silent. I slept a lot of the way and then woke up somewhere over the South Pacific islands—Guadalcanal, Tarawa, Iwo Jima. *Somewhere down there, the foxhole switch happened*, I thought to myself. *I'm closer to that bloody, random night then I've ever been, closer than anyone in my family has ever been.* For a moment, in the shadow light and slumber of the quiet fuselage, the hairs on my arm stood up. I got chills. I was close to him. I was close to that event. My grandfather had come to this part of the world to kill people for the future of a free society. I was now coming here to save an orphan and become a father. The weight of history and irony was once again heavy on my heart. I didn't want to be here. I wanted to be on a stage somewhere; that was my comfort zone. But I knew in my soul that I was supposed to be here. It was the real destiny I didn't want to accept. Flying over the South Pacific was just another ironic message from God: "My poetry is higher and deeper than yours."

ORPHAN'S LULLABY

When an American gets off the plane in China, the culture shock is instant. The first thing you notice is the absolute mass of humanity—bodies upon bodies. In every nook and corner of every building, in all available space in and outdoors, is a human being. You start to see how the value of one human life could get diminished in this sea of flesh, blood, and bone. There, of course, is the ever-present military. There are young Asian men with guns and ill-fitting uniforms looking very stern and serious about all these people in this airport. The next stark reality is that of the food choices: rows and rows of dead, headless snakes (despite the missing heads, still completely intact) lying on ice. All of us Americans, raised going to clean, tidy supermarkets where everything is wrapped in plastic and boxed in cardboard and who are so removed from the up-close brutality of how food actually becomes food, were visibly taken aback by the rawness of dead animals—snakes, fish, foul—simply killed and placed on the shelf, ready for public consumption. There were boxes of food with Chinese writing on them everywhere.

"What is this stuff? How is it made? There's no FDA over here. If the snakes are just killed and placed on these shelves, what else is going on in this country with food?" I asked myself. A wave of nausea engulfed me.

"Oh, dear God, Regie. This is gross," Yolanda said in her most dramatic tone. "What are we going to eat over here?" Mr. and Mrs. Healthy would be in for a challenge.

A walk through the Guangzhou airport to the Beijing connection should be easy. Well, maybe not. The Chinese economy, while centrally planned and communistic, has seemed to produce every scam known to man. A young man in a suit saw the Americans coming. Americans are seen as little walking banks over there. Everybody knows you're there to buy a baby. Everybody knows you have a lot of money on your person. So while they might publicly offer lip service to Mao and the state, all their little inner capitalists are in full bloom. He approached us and said, "You need get to Beijing?" with a sweet, innocent smile and severely broken accent.

"Yes. Which way?" one of us replied.

"I take you to gate; fi dolla each." We all looked at each other. We'd all been swindled before; we were Americans, for Pete's sake, and had probably all bought a used car at one time or another. But we also realized we couldn't read Chinese, and he kind of had us at a disadvantage. We threw knowing smiles at each other and ponied up the cash. Once the young man in the nice suit had his money, he began leading us. We walked and walked and walked and walked—up stairs and down corridors, through terminals and past ticket counters. Finally ending up in the basement somewhere, the young man said, "You keep walking down dat way; you run right in to it." As we looked around and chatted about this, the young man disappeared. Feeling an ambush coming on, we all started quickly walking back toward the light and the upstairs part of the terminal almost by instinct. In the nick of time, one of the families found the right flight (I can't remember how). Our introduction to the land of Buddhism and harmonious living had been a second-rate con artist. We could've gotten that in New York. In a strange way, though, that little scam made me feel at home, and I smiled to myself. *People are the same everywhere*, I thought. *That kid's trying to turn a buck just like me. He's got dreams too. In his country, scamming lost Americans might be the only way he can get close to making them come true. My song was right. The whole world is dreaming* American Dreams.

The bottom of your shoe is a place not to be touched or rubbed on your face. This is an axiom we learn as toddlers. In China, it is an imperative truth. I've never in my life seen so much pollution and disgusting ground cover. It seems like we were constantly walking through some sort of soupy, discolored swill. The rubber soles of my Chinese-made Nike walking shoes were perpetually wet and disgusting. It was only later that I learned of the potty practices of the children in China. Split pants are what the children wear from infancy until they learn how to use a toilet. Unlike our Western diaper system, the children in China simply go to the bathroom in the street through the split pants. It creates an interesting landscape. If the snakes weren't enough, this new hygienic revelation ensured that I would barely eat for the next three weeks. When I landed in China, I weighed 175 pounds. Three weeks later, I would weigh 160. Unfortunately, the weight loss would come from several sources.

The tickle in my throat was getting worse. I had written it off as some sort of sinus thing, but now I was coughing a lot. Everywhere we went, people were wearing surgical masks and trying to ward off the onset of SARS. There was panic back in the States. Here in Asia, they were taking it all in stride, but with every coughing episode, the stares got more and more solemn.

The other families in our group were visibly keeping their distance. Every night at dinner, it was amusing to watch them look for the seat farthest away from me, like a subtle version of duck, duck goose. As the cough got worse, I was getting scared. Had all the trepidation about coming to China actually been the voice of God trying to keep me safe and sound back the U.S.? Was that voice I was hearing telling me not to get on the plane actually one of reason? Had I walked into a catastrophe on the other side of the world? Once again, I couldn't get a handle on my emotions. The health nut guy who refused to eat half the stuff on the menu and who was taking constant doses of vitamin C was the only guy in the group deteriorating. My nutrition witness was being dismantled cough by cough. Surely this thing would pass soon. Surely my new and improved body wouldn't give way to this mysterious, Asian-born death virus. As everything with this journey, the answer to those questions would be abstract at best.

The days in Beijing were filled with bus rides to famous tourist locals and spending disposable American greenbacks on the trinkets and souvenirs the Chinese seem so adept at making. Tiananmen Square, the Forbidden City, and more ancient pagodas than you can reasonably take in, in three days had us almost at the end of our tourism rope. There was one thing left: the Great Wall. You have to see that one. It's a wonder of the world and can be seen from space (so they say. I have no reason to doubt them. How would we know?). So on our last day in Beijing, we made the famous climb. It was truly amazing, I have to say. I called my brother from the top of the lookout post. It was one of the coolest moments of my life. I was sure that one had importance. After climbing the wall and buying all manner of *tchotchkes* for our families back home (at the gift shops you just happened to be forced to walk through to get to your bus), we made our way back to the hotel. On a buzzing, crowded street, the bus stopped somewhere to get lunch or see some famous building or allow us to buy yet more unnecessary stuff. Yolanda and I were shopped out, but we did see something interesting. There was one lone guy standing on the street corner with a kiosk full of little hats that read, "2008 Beijing Olympics." Before that moment, I hadn't realized Beijing had gotten the bid for the '08 games. It was of moderate interest to the whole bus, and many of us bought the hats as almost a gag of sorts. When we were all back on the bus and on the final stretch to the hotel, we began talking about our little girls and how old they would be in 2008. Five years old, maybe six. The subject of coming back to the games in five years and showing the little ones their birthplace became the topic of discussion. Yolanda and I had been accustomed to traveling anywhere we'd wanted to go for the past few years. We had a platinum card filled with frequent flyer miles. We had no travel restrictions in our life and had no reason to believe we would have in 2008. As the conversation solidified, so did the plans. Yolanda said, squeezing my hand, "It's settled! In 2008, we're bringing Isabella back here to see China and watch the Olympic games. Let's all make sure to keep in touch and stay on this." The hats were kitsch. The sentiment was warm. The moment was random. However, that one random moment on a bus in Beijing, China, would one day prove to be a revelation of God's faithfulness and grand design to me. That offhanded little moment would hold secrets and puzzles and riddles I will spend the rest of my life figuring out. The moment at the top of the wall had been cool. The moment in this bus on a street corner in Beijing would one day be divine.

After Beijing, we flew to Guangzhou and linked up with the rest of the twenty-six families at the China hotel and began getting instructions and briefings from our adoption agency. It was almost "gotcha day," as they call it. Emotions were high, and nerves were on edge. Most of us were new parents. Not many of us had any idea what to expect. Yolanda and I certainly didn't. We would spend our last full night without children in a hotel room while I coughed my lungs out. I wish I could've slept. I wish I could've savored the quiet. I had no idea what sinister horrors could be brought on by an eight-month-old baby. The world as I knew it was about to crumble, and a little Chinese girl would push the pillars. In the throes of continual coughing, I got scared, really scared, and called the American embassy. I was starting to believe I might have this SARS thing. We were to fly to Nan Chung the next morning to get Isabella. I wanted to find out the protocol for someone in my condition. The strained exchange with the person on the other end of the phone at the embassy (who spoke broken English at best) was filled with "say that again" and "I'm sorry. Could you repeat that?" But once I fully explained my situation, that I was an American about to adopt a little girl but had all the symptoms of this mysterious illness, SARS, the embassy worker became succinct and clear: "Under no circumstances are you to get on another plane in China until you have a clean bill of health." I hung up the phone and stared at the ground for a minute. What do I do now? Yolanda entered the room, and I told her the news. With a steady fever and unrelenting cough, I was a physical wreck. I was a mental and emotional one as well. With clammy hands holding my throbbing, sweaty head, I asked, "What do we do, Yolanda? Should I stay here? I'm just confused." She'd had enough of my whining. She'd been nursing me through the conflict with career versus family. The tortured artist thing had finally run its course with her. She verbally lunged into me like a tigress. The cursed vein popped out in her neck, the one you just never, ever want to see. "I can't adopt this baby without you! You're sick, but we have no idea if she is sick. Stop making phone calls. Stop worrying about things you can't change. I need you to get up, pack your stuff, and get your whiny butt on that plane tomorrow." As she left the room, I could feel the eye roll.

Pack my stuff I did; get my whiny butt on the plane I also did. By six o'clock that afternoon, I would be a father, but I was still focused on myself and my own ailments. At this point, my career had vanished into the distance; I was simply worried about surviving China and getting home. The translator and guide assigned to us had instructed me not to go to the hospital at any cost. "If you have SARS, they will quarantine you, and you may never get home. If you don't have SARS, they'll still quarantine you with those who do have it because of your symptoms. You'll get it there if you don't have it now. Either way, if you go to the hospital; it could be months before you get home, if you ever get back there at all." Wow. Thanks for that little heaven muffin. Nothing like being casually told how your death might come about in a foreign land by someone who is moderately interested at best. My brain was in full panic and my body in full turmoil. The wheels were down in Nan Chung, and a baby was two hours away.

It was a twisting, turning, hot, and exhausting hour-and-a-half bus ride to the hotel—thirty minutes to baby! We had just enough time to get to our rooms and unpack. There was no time for showers or unwinding. There were children waiting on new parents. It was time to be grown up. The babies had been traveling on gravel roads in a van for six hours. They would be hot, hungry, and exhausted. Some would even be sick. I knew how they felt. Once we were in the room, I went into an uncontrollable coughing fit. I couldn't stop. It went on for minutes, and I even threw up a little toward the end. "Should I even go to this?" I asked Yolanda. "I'm not sure I should be handling the baby; I don't want to get her sick." I actually wasn't kidding; I was freaked out.

"You don't have SARS. Come get your daughter," was Yolanda's response. I washed my hands and face, grabbed the video camera, and walked to the elevator.

Every heart on the elevator was pounding. We were silent, nervously smiling, and trying to be reasonably calm. Some had their eyes closed in what appeared to be silent prayer. Most parents receive their children in hospitals surrounded by doctors and family. For most, it is a solitary moment for them and them only. We would be receiving our children in a strange assembly line, like kids waiting on Santa to pass them a toy at the school Christmas party. No privacy and nothing singular about it. There were fifteen families huddled at the hotel elevator landing. When each name was called, they would step to the front of the group and a squirmy little bundle with a little patch of black hair would be brought to them and placed in their arms. It was surreal to watch couple after couple have their first moments with their child in front of everyone. They would burst into tears and begin saying things to the little one. The babies were confused by the whole ordeal, and by the time the third baby had been given, the place sounded like a full-fledged orphanage. Number six: Regie and Yolanda Hamm. We walked forward. I was trying to conceal my coughs and keep a straight face. Heart pounding, head pounding, flushed face, sweaty palms. Yolanda squeezed my hand; here she came. She was asleep and motionless. As the caregiver got closer and closer, I started to make her features out: two beautifully closed almond-shaped eyes, a full, pouty little mouth, adorable patch of black hair on her small head. She was placed in Yolanda's arms, and the tears burst forth uncontrollably. Yolanda engulfed her in her arms and showered her baby head with kisses. She rocked her back and forth in motherly affection, talking baby talk the way only mommies can, then looked over at me, and placed the baby in my arms. Something strange happened to me in that moment. In one nanosecond, I stopped caring about my own health. I couldn't feel the tickle in my lungs. My fever had numbed. I couldn't remember where my single was on the charts. All of my energy was refocused on this little thing sleeping on my chest, the most beautiful thing I'd ever seen in my life. The minute her little body touched mine, everything in my life was realigned. Now, nothing else mattered but her.

Yolanda, being the instant mom she was, felt Isabella's head and said, "This baby has a fever." She did indeed. We were told that the babies had all gotten fresh immunizations before making the trip to the hotel and that was probably the reason for the fever. We took it in stride, rejoiced with the other families, cooed over all the other babies, and then went to the debriefing. In that meeting, Isabella's caregiver told us that she took six bottles a day, liked loud noises, and slept twelve hours a night with no trouble. This stunningly beautiful specimen of a baby also seemed to have an easy-going personality. We were blessed. We hugged the caregiver and took our new bundled treasure back to the room to begin the business of getting to know her.

She was out of it but still sort of bothered it seemed. That precious scowl was in full force. We walked into the room slowly. Yolanda was holding her and whispering quiet baby talk. "That's a sweet girl now. Hers has got the sleepies and don't know what's going on. Who are these crazy people anyway? They look funny to me. I know, sweet girl, I know." I was leaning over her as well, kissing her forehead and wrapping her tiny fingers around mine. This moment had officially surpassed every moment I'd ever had in my life. Of all the wonderful things that have happened to me (and there have been many), being alone with my wife and daughter for the first time as a family was such a profound moment that it changed everything about me from that day to this. I separate my life into two parts: BC and AC, before children and after children. The weight of the responsibility wasn't heavy, but it was profound. On April 1, 2003, I became a grown-up—and made another small surrender. We gently placed her on the bed and began loosening the hodgepodge of clothes that bound her. There were two or three different layers. Apparently the Chinese are obsessed with children not getting cold. I've never seen so many bundled-up kids in my life. After we were finally through all the layers, we began inspecting her tiny body. Her toenails were dirty and growing sideways from wearing shoes too small . As we inspected her feet more closely, we found several fresh needle marks. What in the world had happened to this child? The cold air was making her chill. We filled the bathroom sink with warm water and placed her in it. She began screaming at the top of her lungs as if she were dying.

"What do we do, Regie?" Yolanda yelled at me.

"I don't know. I don't even know what's going on. Why is she suddenly crying? She was sleeping two seconds ago!" Later, upon talking with other couples, we realized she'd probably never had anything other than a sponge bath and was freaked out by the water. She would learn to love it in a matter of days. After cleaning her up, we tried to give her a bottle, but she wouldn't eat. She lay limp and sleeping. We decided to let her sleep for a while and try again later; we were certain she was just traumatized, and with enough time, she'd come around. It would be the first of many incorrect assumptions.

We'd heard from friends who had adopted Chinese babies that they would sometimes sleep for the first twenty-four hours due to exhaustion or extreme emotional trauma. I mean, after all, these tiny babies, who had probably never been in a room by themselves in their entire existence, were now isolated and quiet, surrounded by people who looked so different from all the people they were used to seeing. I remember thinking these little girls must feel like they've been abducted by aliens. What a shock to the system. Although Isabella had a fever, we were convinced the trauma of the whole day would eventually wear off and she would get back to normal. But her fever was climbing, and she wasn't getting better at all. By that evening, we knew we had to get fluids down her, but she wouldn't take a bottle. It was as if she'd never had one and didn't understand the concept. Finally, we hit upon the idea of putting formula in a medicine dropper and shooting it down her throat. It worked. She wasn't happy about it, but we were able to get several ounces of formula into her tiny belly. I would sit on the bed with my knees up and then place her on my knees with her head facing me. The feeding ritual would take at least an hour each time, but it was working. This would go on for days. She simply wouldn't take a bottle. Had someone been breast feeding her in the orphanage? We'd heard rumors that some of the foster workers would breast feed and then take the state subsidy for baby formula and pocket it. Given our encounters with the Chinese, we were inclined to believe that had happened in Isabella's case. Convinced we were now weaning a child off breast milk, we cursed some poor nameless, faceless woman often. You look for reasons. This one was plausible.

Two days and Isabella hadn't taken a bottle, and her fever hadn't gone down. Incidentally, mine hadn't either. We were both in bad shape. I had sort of forgotten about my problems in the wake of her issues. Now, the whole thing was getting a little frightening. Yolanda was out and working the problem, going to the hotel doctor to make an appointment and maybe bring back some medicine, talking with the translators and agency workers about options, going from room to room, asking about formula, bottle nipples, etc. Isabella and I were laying in bed, both with a fever, both out of it. As I lay there, the weight of the situation fell on me. I had seen the hotel doctor in Guangzhou. She said she wasn't sure what I had and gave me some Chinese medicine in the form of a coffee drink. It turned out to be something like an espresso with loads of sugar. Since I hadn't had sugar in over a year, it basically gave me a temporary high, followed by one of the worst migraine headaches of my life. The room was starting to spin. They weren't going to figure out what I had in this country, let alone cure it. If I could just get back to America, this would all be okay. On that sick bed, I realized what a beacon America is to the world. All my thoughts were drifting toward a place of hope and answers. Here, there seemed to be very little of either, and this little girl I'd known for all of two days might have the same illness as me. I looked at her. She was angelic, beautiful, almost sacred. I started crying uncontrollably. This was my daughter. She had been a picture, a concept, an inconvenience, a catalyst, an expense, a miracle. Now she was flesh and blood and mine. Sweat beading on my head, running down my face to mix with the tears and soaking the sheets, I reached over and touched her tiny hand. In that moment, I didn't believe I would ever leave China alive. I had deteriorated so much; I just couldn't see myself getting better. I was going to die here with this little girl who never knew me by my side. "Boy dreams American dreams. Dies in China" was the headline I kept seeing. I thought about my mother and father and all the years of being on the road with them. I thought about my brother and how much I loved him. I thought about my wife, her incredible strength and all that I'd put her through. Caressing my little Isabella's hand, I reconciled it all right there. For the first time, I was content to simply be Isabella's daddy and die with her in China. I smiled through the tears. This would be okay. God would embrace us. I was ready. I was blessed. None of it mattered anymore. Lying next to her, I wrote a song:

You were born under the China sun,
And I was born in America, down where the rebels run.
Some strange and lovely road led me to your arms.
I'm still not real sure how, but, baby, here we are.
Worlds can collide, girl,
But sometimes they embrace.
I found my world
In the smile on your angel face.
Love ain't no man's land, sure ain't made of stone.
Love is heart, love is soul, love is home.
I packed my bags and came so far for you.
They call you a lucky baby. Well, baby, I'm lucky too
'Cause you gave me brand-new dreams with just one
photograph
So I'd fly ten thousand miles just to hear you laugh.
Worlds can collide, girl,
But sometimes they embrace.
I found my world
In the smile on your angel face.
Love ain't no man's land, sure ain't made of stone
Love is heart, love is soul, love is home.

Yolanda burst in the door. "We've got to get this baby to the hospital. Can you go, or do I need to go without you?" Drying my eyes, I said, "I'm fine. Let's go." I washed my face, dressed, and tried to shake off my aches and trembling body. We bundled our little mystery and were out the door for a cab. Standing at the hotel entrance with the translator, we saw other families in our group strolling with their babies around the hotel grounds. Some had already adjusted to their new parents and were laughing and cooing. Happy mommies and daddies were baby talking to the black-haired China dolls. My eyes were fixed. "Let's go, Reg," said Yolanda. I was in the cab and back to reality. The translator barked out mandarin orders to the cab driver; we practically screeched out of the hotel entrance into the impossible Nan Chung traffic. Though Nan Chung is roughly the size of Chicago, it's a relatively medium-sized city for China. To my American eyes, it was nothing short of a Mad Max film. All manner of humanity was buzzing about in some type of chaotic harmony. Cars were almost hitting each other and then veering off just in the nick of time. Busses headed straight for us and then swerved just before impact. I'd been around this for a week already, but now my senses were more heightened with this new baby to protect. Yolanda held her close and tight like a fragile treasure. We were racing through the streets to the state hospital. The city looked gray, depressed, and lost in time. Oddly named cars (not normally seen in the U.S) packed the streets, along with just as many bicycles and pedestrians passing small, dingy little diners and businesses that all ran together. The colors were all sepia into a brownish hue under the constant drizzle of rain. I felt like I was caught somewhere in the 1940s.

The grayish white edifice looked nice enough from the road. Stately and official, the government-run hospital was our stop. We exited the cab, paid our fare, and began walking the little one in. The translator told us to follow her lead and let her handle all the formalities. The outside of the building had deceived us. There was no roof on most of the building. Entering the front door, the open-air structure was cavernous and sparse. Gray plaster walls reaching upwards of thirty to forty feet on all sides were cracking and spotted, the paint fading. Armed soldiers were posted at the corners. In the center of the prisonlike compound was the information station. On each side of it was a eight-inch trough spanning the width of the building with water running through it. *Interesting drainage*, I thought to myself. Interesting indeed. A minute later, I noticed a state worker pushing squeegee after squeegee of fluid into these troughs. "Oh my. Yolanda, that's human waste." I looked down and realized the floors were angled so the run-off would gather in the troughs and run out of the building to God knows where. I was videotaping. This was all surreal. Americans hardly ever get access to communist Chinese hospitals. I was getting an education. Several times, guards motioned me to put the camera down. This wasn't something they wanted shown on Oprah. Whenever a guard would walk toward me, I would put the camera back on Isabella (or another child waiting) and act like a silly, tourist father.

We waited in the urine-smelling room for what seemed like an eternity. Sarah (our translator) came and got us. We would now go to the diagnosis room. We walked the length of the open-air structure, stepped over the waste trough, and rounded the corner. As we entered the room, the sight made me almost lightheaded. You can hear me on the video say to Yolanda, "Yolanda, is this what I think it is? Am I seeing this right?" There were rows and rows of children with IVs in their heads. I'd never seen a scalp IV; every kid in that gray, echoing, condemned-feeling building had a scalp IV. Sarah explained that scalp IVs were more efficient and got the medicine into the patient sooner. We stood in the diagnosis line while we stared at these children screaming and writhing with needles in their heads. Soon we were up and walked toward what appeared to be a teller window. Two nurses wearing masks and who were clearly exhausted were standing behind the glass. There was a two-foot opening at the bottom of the glass where they would perform their services. The gray, three-foot-by-three-foot mat where we would lay Isabella was littered with bloody gauze and some type of mucus. While they were trying to lay Isabella down on it, Yolanda was feverishly sweeping off the gauze and wiping the mat down with the handy wipes from Isabella's bag. The nurses didn't seem too concerned with hygiene.

I looked down to realize the bloody gauze had been piling up on the floor all day; it was everywhere. Americans are just not seen in these hospitals. This is the health care system reserved for the Chinese masses that might never see a real, live American their entire lives. We were quickly becoming zoo animals.

As the DMV-style nurses held my daughter down and drew blood from her, she began screaming. It was the first sign of life we'd seen from her in days. While helping to hold her and reassure her, I noticed people getting closer and closer to us. They wanted to see us up close. There was screaming and Chinese chatter and all manner of chaos around me. No personal space whatsoever. Soon, I heard a voice cut through the rest. My head pounding from a coughing attack, wiping sweat from my neck, I turned to see the little Chinese woman. She looked like a Hollywood stereotype: brown peasant clothes, work boots, dirty face with a bandana wrapped around her head. She had indiscriminant scars on her face and hands that spoke of a life much harder than mine. She was barking Chinese at me at the speed of light. Smiling politely and nodding, I would periodically turn from her screaming to attend to my own daughter's screaming. When I turned back again, she had placed her three-year-old son on the table next us and was grabbing his face, turning it from side to side, opening his mouth, and showing off his teeth. When I went to turn back to Isabella, she grabbed my arm. I turned back. Smiling, I made the I-don't-understand-you motion. Sarah intervened and began speaking to the woman. After a quick exchange, Sarah leaned into me and yelled over the noise, "She wants you to take her son back to America and raise him there."

I thought she was joking. "Oh no, we have our hands full here," I said, pointing and smiling at my screaming daughter.

"She's not kidding," Sarah said. "I'm trying to explain to her how it works. She's just never been this close to an American, and she's taking a chance for her son."

I stared at the little boy and his mother. The quiet, defeated father was behind them, smoking a cigarette. One of the perks of communist China: you can still smoke in the hospital. The father was smiling a toothless smile at me and nodding as if to say, "Take him. He's a good boy; he'll work real hard." The people of China were lovely and graceful and accommodating and desperate. They knew there was a better life somewhere, and they were willing to give up their children for their children to have it. I see this woman in my dreams to this day, but before I had a chance to even give her another look, we were whisked off to another room. Word was out that Americans were here. We were being walked to the front of the line.

We walked up two flights of stairs, past rooms full of people, to another set of bank teller windows. This is where you received the results of the tests they took at the other set of bloody bank teller windows. They called us up.

"She has virus," the doctor said.

"What kind?" I asked. "Does she have SARS? Ask him, Sarah. Ask him if it's SARS," I said in Sarah's ear.

"Virus!" he said staunchly. "Just virus. She get antibiotic now." His angry, militant tone made me want to click my heels and give the Hitler salute. We went back down the stairs into the cursed treatment room. This was the room I'd seen with horror two hours earlier. We were at yet another teller window, and this time Isabella would be receiving one of those patented scalp IVs. Isabella screamed. It made my stomach hurt. Suddenly, her head began to swell. "Dear God, what's happening?" Yolanda half-screamed. They'd put the IV in wrong, and fluid was building up. They pulled the needle out, let it drain, and started again. More screaming. Finally, something came over Isabella. She quieted and surrendered. She stared at me with the most peaceful, serene look. There was no point in flailing. Let it happen. We sat in a chair with her as the antibiotic seeped into her head. When the bag was empty, they quickly and unceremoniously pulled the scalp IV and sent us on our way. I kept asking Sarah if we had any prescriptions to fill and if not, why not. One big antibiotic dose wasn't good for you. I quickly learned that they don't taper antibiotics off in China. You get your dose and go home. The holes in Isabella's feet now made sense. She'd been given several IVs already that week. They just kept taking her back. The logic of state-controlled medicine can get a little hazy. Isabella needed monitored doses of antibiotics. She didn't need a two-hour IV drip and then nothing. As we thought might happen, we were back again the next day. There would be more urine in the trough and bloody gauze on the floor. There would be more cattle call medicine, more children screaming, and another scalp IV for my precious girl. She wasn't legally ours yet. We had no choice but to do what the state required until we got on that plane back to the States. The good news was we were going back to Guangzhou the next day. If we could get her well enough to travel, maybe things would get better there.

By the end of the week, Isabella's fever had broken for a while. She was awake and relatively alert, but she was a rag doll. She couldn't sit up or even hold her head steady. The first night we took her to dinner, I sat her on my lap and tried to feed her. She was limp and sliding, wobbling and toppling. Her head wouldn't remain straight, and eating food was completely out of the question. While I sat there trying to balance her and keep her stable, I looked up to see all the other parents at the round, family-style table staring at me. Was I doing something wrong? This had to be my fault. I wasn't doing this right. All these other little girls were eating and smiling, and some were even walking. My

Isabella couldn't hold her head up and would barely take a bottle. I knew I wasn't cut out for this. *I'm a terrible father!* I thought to myself. I excused myself, took Isabella back to the room, and once again got the medicine dropper ready. What was wrong with me? What was wrong with my little girl?

The next day, we pulled it together well enough to get through the slog of government agencies and red tape in Nan Chung. We entered room after room and sat in front of desk after desk. We smiled and bowed to countless government officials, filled out pages and pages of documents and affidavits, and received stamp after official stamp. I'd been carrying Isabella all day in one of those reverse backpack things that holds the baby on your chest. I'd been making up lullabies and trying to keep her quiet and calm, petting and kissing her head. By the end of the day, we were all three sweaty and spent. We went back to the hotel. One more night here and then we would get back on a plane to Guangzhou. We were by no means out of the woods, but at this point were just focused on getting back to the States. We still had faith that all would be solved on American soil. Two weeks and my cough had not subsided in the least. There would be one last night in Nan Chung, China, and it would be the last full night of sleep Yolanda, Isabella, or I would have for the next four years.

In the next morning we packed, went to breakfast, fed Isabella with the medicine dropper, changed her diaper, carried our overstuffed bags to the lobby of the hotel, and climbed on another bus to another airport. This time we were carrying a baby, and the travel was slower and every movement was much more deliberate. Navigating the airport was now moving at an excruciating pace. Bottles and diapers and every shaker toy and stuffed animal known to man now hindered our once well-honed and effortless travel skills. We lumbered through the ticket and bag check lines onto the awaiting jet that would carry us away from this place forever. We boarded, settled, and belted in. Soon, there was movement, sweet movement. Suddenly there was speed and lift and wheels off the ground. As I watched Nan Chung get smaller through my window, I knew I would never be back in that city again for the rest of my life, and yet it would always be with me.

I thought about a three-year-old boy and his parents. I stared at my little rag doll. There was one week left in China. *I can hold on one more week.* Isabella was quiet and still, and Yolanda and I exhaled. For a moment, we were all three silent and calm. Three hours later the wheels would touch down in Guangzhou again. All twenty-six families would reconvene at the China hotel. Some had adopted from Guang Dong, some from right there in Guangzhou. We were all back together for one last week of bureaucracy and red (literally) tape; then the little girls would finally be ours. Another day of stressful checking in and getting settled. Then came the night.

I had gone to dinner while Yolanda stayed with the baby. Around 10:00 p.m., I got in the elevator (carrying Yolanda's meal in a box) and went up to our floor. As the doors opened, I heard the strangest cry I had yet heard from any of the babies. It was piercing the hallway. *Oh great, one of these kids has decided to cry all night,* I thought to myself. As I got closer to our room, I walked slower. This couldn't be mine. She slept all the time and was very quiet. I opened the door to see Yolanda sitting up staring at me. "That's ours?" I said in disbelief.

"Oh yes. She's been doing this for about an hour now. She's not sleeping more than an hour at a time."

"You think she's still sick?" I said.

"Well, she has no fever. I'm thinking this baby is just tired and still traumatized from the week."

Ten turned to midnight. Midnight turned to 3:00 a.m. Isabella would sleep for an hour, maybe an hour and a half at a time. She would wake up with this strange catlike cry. It was eerie and unsettling, and it was happening like clockwork. I know it had to be keeping others in the hotel up as well. She was loud. By 6:00 a.m., Yolanda decided to go to the gym. I walked the floor with Isabella until she returned. Two hours of TV and pampering had settled the baby down. She was now quietly lying on the bed next to me, propped up and surrounded by pillows. The key was in the lock; Yolanda walked in.

"I'm going to shower and then give the baby a bath. Maybe that'll make her feel better, and she can sleep a little." Because Isabella couldn't sit up, Yolanda had to sit in the bathtub with her. I would be in charge of getting her ready for the bath and then bring her to the tub. I stripped her down and was carrying her to the bathroom. I stopped for a second and then kind of tossed her up in the air a little. "Whee. Look at you flying, Isabella," I said in my goofiest baby voice. With her naked body airborne, she began laughing hysterically. It was the first time she had smiled since we'd had her. I laughed and cried. Coughing and wheezing, I tossed her up again. She laughed again. I cried again. Yolanda darted around the corner. "Is she laughing?"

"Yep. Apparently she's a little adrenaline junky," I said, tossing her gently upward. The baby cackle was sweet and infectious. Yolanda began laughing and crying too. From that moment on, making Isabella laugh became my number one mission in life. That precious smile was something I would simply have to experience every day.

With five days left in China and no letup in my cough, I went back to the hotel doctor. This time, it was a different doctor. He was a small, old Chinese man with a squished-up face and hearty smile. "You come. Sit down. I listen to ya lung," he said.

Placing the cold apparatus on my chest, he must've held it there for ten minutes. "Oh. Hm. Okay, okay. Hm. Ah." It was as if he were listening to his first set of lungs ever. "Okay. You, ah, no have a SARS. You a have a bronchitis. Very bad. Very bad bronchitis." At first, I felt relief. Then I remembered hearing about some SARS patients who had been misdiagnosed with bronchitis. I was suddenly gripped with another wave of fear.

"You're sure? Just bronchitis?" I said nervously.

"Oh yes. No, ah, SARS. No a need a medicine. You, ah, need rest, only rest."

Rest, he says. Interesting concept.

The families had all been asking questions about me and my career. We had all become very close in a short period of time. You don't go through things like we'd been through together and not bond. There was a grand piano in the China hotel, and the twenty-six families went to the management staff to ask if I could hold a mini concert in the lobby. Watching communism at work was truly interesting. The playing of the piano had to be cleared with a state agency. The tuning of the piano must be cleared as well. A request and affidavit must be filed on my behalf, along with some sort of voucher from the adoption agency that I would not be subversive in any way. The time slot must be stringently adhered to—fifteen minutes, no more, no less (interestingly enough). A copy of my CD was taken so songs could be approved for performance. It would take several days to clear these things just so I could sit at a piano in a lobby and play three songs. The families and the agency filed the paperwork. I guess they really wanted some entertainment after the week they'd all had. My show was approved for the last day of our stay. I'd come to China to adopt a little girl, and here I was working again. It was the first time in three weeks I'd thought about my career. This would be an interesting set list. I had no written guarantee of freedom of speech here. I couldn't just sing anything I wanted. I decided on "Babies," "American Dreams" (even in China I had a defiant streak), and "Love Is Home," the song I'd written sweating out a fever and holding my baby's tiny hand. Somehow, all three were approved. On the last day there, I would gig in Guangzhou. The nights were unbearable. Once Isabella's fever broke and we were living in the hotel in Guangzhou, she never slept more than two hours without waking up with that horrifying cry. The only good news was my fever was gone and my cough was drying up. I started feeling like I just might make it out of there. Still, why was this child not sleeping? How was she surviving? Yolanda and I were walking zombies. Three days without sleep is horrible. Two more days and we'd be home. Home would solve everything. We just had to make it until then. For now, I had a show to do. I went to the hotel gym and went for my preshow run. It was my first run in three weeks. I made the three miles fairly easily without coughing too much. I could sing. Shower, dressed, elevator, piano—this was home to me. The fifty-some-odd people gathered around me. I put my fingers on the keys and started. At the end of the piano stood Yolanda holding Isabella. As I began to sing, Isabella shook from side to side, laughed, and squealed with abandon. It was probably the first time she'd seen anyone play an instrument up close. She was taken; so was I. I hardly remember a thing about that performance. I know I played a few songs, and the home crowd enjoyed it. I was watching my baby fall in love with music, and I was falling in love with her. We would be music buddies from then on.

The cold, bureaucratic question that haunted me the whole time we were processing our adoption was, "Are you happy with your baby?" Every Chinese official in every office asked this question first. I always wondered what would've happened if we had said, "No, we'd like another one." Everyone who goes to China to adopt hears the urban legends about how the children are strapped down or abused or any number of horrifying things. I personally found the people of China to be extremely loving toward these orphans, and they seemed to want the best for the babies. Still, the extreme humanitarian crisis caused by the sheer numbers of orphans brought with it its own set of mandates. If children were strapped in cribs (and I'm quite certain they were), it would only be because two or three orphanage workers simply cannot attend to sixty or seventy screaming babies all day and all night. The only way to insure they remain safe until they can be attended is by strapping them in their cribs. When you see it up close, it actually makes sense.

One of the hard realities I witnessed first hand was at one of the nicer orphanages in Guangzhou. The Chinese govern-ment prepared a sight–seeing tour through this orphanage as a way of showing us all how well the children had been treated and how state-of-the-art their facilities were. Yolanda begged off and stayed in the bus with the baby. I wanted to see the best case scenario if my daughter hadn't come home with me. As we walked into the open-air pavilion, leading to the front of the edi-fice, children came running at us from our left and landed at a restraining wall just high enough for them to peek over. They were loud and startled us. I walked over to say hi when I heard them all screaming out of sync with each other some phrase I could barely make out. As I got closer, I heard one of them more clearly. "Hello. How are you?" one little boy barked at the top of his lungs. He appeared to have a cleft pallet, and as I scanned the group of kids and smiled and shouted "Ni how" back at them, I noticed a Down syndrome little girl and another little boy walk-ing with a strange gait. Soon it dawned on me I was observ-ing the special needs section of this orphanage. At first glance, the fenced in courtyard in which they were playing looked like a perfectly normal children's playground. Upon closer observation I witnessed a few kids sitting in corners rocking back and forth and still more crawling around on the ground flicking rocks and dirt with their fingers. A clearly exhausted and weathered caregiver sparsely supervised the children. She walked up and informed us this was where the special needs orphans were being raised. Because it's extremely rare for anyone to request a special needs child to adopt, these children would most likely live out their lives in that place, playing in that little corral every day until they were not children anymore. What would happen then? Who knows? Some of them wouldn't survive that long. Maybe some would be high functioning enough to be given a menial job at the orphanage if they were lucky. I would imagine the more profoundly delayed children would be placed in a state run facility for their entire lives. Knowing what I knew about the hospitals and orphanages there, I could only imagine what kind of place that might be. The worker informed us that they had taught the children how to say, "Hello. How are you?" in English. As soon as they heard her say it, they involuntarily chimed in again, yelling, "Hello. How are you?" Upon that second greeting, I was unable to hold back my tears. I reached over the little wall to touch their little heads and hands. I wanted to grab them all up and embrace them and tell them everything was going to be okay. But I knew it wasn't going to be okay, at least not for all of them.

"Are you happy with your baby?" The answer to that question would be a resounding *yes* from here on out. Whatever malady my rag doll possessed was going back to the United States with her daddy and mommy.

LOVE IS HOME

*I*t was our last day in China. There was one more agency to visit. We walked in the room with Isabella and the translator, bowed, and sat. Question after question was posed to us. How far do you plan to continue her education? Will she have her own room? Do you have a house or apartment? What do you do for a living? "I'm a musician," I answered. The translator then had quite a long exchange with the very official-looking lady sitting behind the desk. They were pointing at Isabella and peppering their exchanges with oohs and aahs. What were they talking about? *Great. They don't want a musician adopting a Chinese baby!* I thought to myself. "I should've told them I was in publishing," I said to Yolanda under my breath. That's the official sidestep when you don't want to have the I'm-in-the-music-business conversation with someone. At least in America, telling a stranger you're in the music business is like telling a dog you're in the steak business. Someone is always a songwriter in his spare time or he has a cousin who is simply amazing or his kid is just about to graduate and is looking for someone to help him catch the right break. It's the most annoying thing in the world, and I have become sheepish over the years about discussing what I do with people. It's hard to explain why everyone can't be a superstar and more difficult to explain why I'm not going to drop everything and help him achieve his most-cherished dreams. Surely, this wouldn't follow me to China.

"She say dat you daughter very, very beautiful," the translator suddenly said to us.

"Yes, she is," we replied.

"And, eh, since you American music stah, you make, eh, you daughter American music stah when eh she olda, like, eh, Barittany Speah," the translator explained. I stared in disbelief. I knew these people meant absolutely no harm, but the fact that the worst of American pop culture had so permeated the globe and I was getting this strange request in a country that shunned so many aspects of Western life but chose this aspect as shining example of what should be aspired to bothered me to my core and actually made me wince a little that I was a part of such a machine.

"The Chinese government is asking me to turn my daughter into Britney Spears?" I asked in contempt.

"Yes!" the translator said in an unexpectedly excited way. We just sat there staring at the translator and agency chief as they smiled back at us with big, innocent grins. Yolanda knows me well and knew I was getting indignant. She patted my leg and said, "It's okay, baby" under her breath.

"Isn't that an interesting idea," Yolanda interrupted, squeezing my hand and smiling at me with that don't-get-into-it-here-with-this-woman-Regie smile.

"Well...um...we'll see how it goes. Maybe so," I said with the most sincere smile I could muster while trying to keep my rag doll's head erect. "She's definitely beautiful. Anything can happen." We stood to leave. "In America," I said under my breath as we walked out of the room. "Get me home, Yolanda. I need to get home," I quipped.

"Baby, I'm so with you. Let's get on that plane and never look back." There would be one more sleepless night in China before we got on that homebound plane. We would be up at 10:00 p.m. and again at midnight and again at 3:00 a.m. and yet again at 6:00 a.m. At 8:00 a.m. we shook off the previous night and began the ritual of showers and packing. We once again made our way to the hotel lobby, where we would be begin another day of more busses and more paper work to complete. My cough had finally subsided right in the nick of time. There were reports of the government not allowing people on flights out of China with coughs. Everyone in the group had been pulling for me. They were all visibly relieved when I could talk to them for more than a minute without barking. Walking the maze that is leaving one country and flying to another, we were all terribly excited to get home. The guards in the airport seemed peeved. We were leaving their country with some of their people; I couldn't tell if they understood or cared or were just angry in general. Some of those little girls may have been fathered by some of those soldiers. It was all very mysterious to me. This country of so many people and yet so much secrecy was an enigma to me. I was ready to get back to the U.S., back to my family and friends, back to my beautiful house, back to things, people, and language I understood, back to my career. Boarding was painstakingly slow. There were tears, opened suitcases inspected indiscriminately, passports, lines, bottles, diaper changes, lines, hugs good-bye to translators, boarding passes, lines, doors closed, seat belts on, instructions, movement, sweet movement, speed, and finally the wheels were up; next stop: LA.

This was a night flight. It would be done completely under the cover of darkness while the sun was on the other side of the world. All the parents were settling the babies in for a long nap. At cruising altitude, the cabin was quiet and cozy with only the hum of the engines in the background. Isabella was sleeping when we took off; that wouldn't last long. My rag doll came to life just as all the other little girls were getting droopy-eyed. Suddenly, the screaming started. Yolanda tried rocking her. It worked for about ten minutes, just long enough for all the little girls to fall back asleep. Then there came that strange cry. It was the unwelcome alarm clock for all twenty-six Chinese babies in the cabin, and they began crying as well. We were getting the looks from the other families. You know, the keep-that-brat-quiet looks. We tried everything—rocking, patting, whispering, walking her upright, walking her sideways, giving her a bottle (which she'd finally started taking), shaking toys in her face, massaging her legs, everything. Nothing worked. Finally, I put the backward backpack on and hoisted her into it. We made a little trail up to the first class section and then back again. She smiled and fell asleep against my chest. Thinking she was out, I tried to hand her to Yolanda. No dice. The scream started again and set off a chain of events that produced scowls and anger from the other parents imprisoned on this plane filled with volatile children. My rag doll awakened the other sleeping babies, and one scream suddenly became many. I put her back in the pack and continued my monotonous march from one end of the plane to the other. Every time I tried to put her down, she screamed. The only thing that was working was me walking the floor with her. When Yolanda tried, it evoked more screams. So, for about ten of the fourteen hours in the air, I walked up and down the aisles of the China Air cabin. I was already exhausted from the week, and this was throwing me into full range fatigue. My legs hurt, my back hurt, and I was sweating from her body heat. Even with the constant walking, she still woke up about every other hour and had a crying fit. Families were finding other seats on the plane. I was trying to keep her as quiet as possible, but that cry, that strange, inexplicable cry, wouldn't subside. Home wasn't getting here fast enough. How much of this could I take? I had never been pushed so close to the edge of my own breaking point. Surely being home would lighten this burden. For this long, miserable night, however, I would be pushed as far as I ever had been. It was strange torture.

I woke with a start. About an hour before landing, Yolanda had taken the baby from me, and we'd all fallen mercifully asleep. The bell that signaled final descent had shaken me loose from some dream. "Ladies and gentlemen, prepare for landing" were the words we'd all been waiting to hear for weeks. An audible gasp brushed through the cabin and the excitement was mounting.

"Ladies and gentlemen, the CDC has been informed of a passenger with troubling symptoms and will be escorting him off the plane upon landing. Please remain seated while we contact the passenger." Oh God! They found me! Yolanda grabbed my hand. Every person in our area craned their necks around to look directly at me. One of the new fathers behind me leaned up and said, "Dude, I thought you were in the clear. Hang in there, man." My heart was pounding. I was wiping my eyes and trying to get coherent as the wheels touched down and we taxied to the gate. Were they coming for me? I was almost certain of it. Just then, two women in surgical masks boarded the plane and made a beeline for the back. I watched with my heart in my throat as they escorted an Asian man off the plane who was coughing uncontrollably. Wow. What kind of protocol had taken over in the States while we were gone? The only news we'd seen was communist China TV and the BBC. As our tour guide in Beijing had so aptly put it, "Once the government took over the news media, we started getting only good news." A steady diet of (good) Chinese news and the BBC had left me thinking SARS was no big deal and the U.S was being pushed out of Iraq by Saddam Hussein. I wasn't sure if I truly had the correct information. Had SARS become Armageddon in the States? Would I be quarantined in LA?

"Ladies and gentlemen, please remain seated while the CDC passes out this information booklet that will give you behavioral guidelines for the next ten days." We sat another twenty minutes and received our little booklets. They could've told us all this in about thirty seconds. Don't go anywhere. Don't kiss anybody. Wash your hands every hour. Stay in your house for the next ten days. We were about to, once again, completely disregard CDC recommendations, and it still wouldn't be the last time.

I had been in China for three weeks, and I never saw the sun. Although I'd been oriented to believe my country was the great polluting Satan of the world, it seemed to me that China was the most polluted place I'd ever seen. The skies were always overcast, even in sunlight. The haze that hung over every city I visited was stifling. There were ordinances against running outside in Guangzhou because of unsafe air quality. This is why my one and only preshow run had been on a treadmill in a high rise and not through some city-planned walking trail. The air quality inside was better than it was outside. Walking off the plane in LA, I felt like breathing again. I've always seen LA as a bit of a cesspool. The smog, traffic, and graffiti make it look like a once-golden metropolis gone awry. Still, after returning from China, I wanted to kiss the California ground. LA looked healthy and pristine for the first time in my life. I was in America again, and that meant hope.

We waited in the terminal for over an hour, standing with these exhausted, sweaty babies, for customs to come out and magically make the babies into citizens of the U.S. There would be more paperwork, more swearing in in courtrooms, more bureaucracy, but for now (with the wave of one customs agent's hand), the babies were officially ours and in the United States of America legally. There were tears of relief all through the long passport lines. We hugged and took pictures and said bittersweet good-byes to the families with whom we'd shared this amazing adventure. Now, it was over, and we were off to start our new lives with these children. Eventually, everyone dispersed, and we, once again, found ourselves in the mundane rituals of baggage claim, hailing cabs, and checking into another hotel. We would be in LA one night and then head home to Tennessee the next day. I'm a Southern boy, and I longed for home. When I started having success in pop music, some told me I should relocate to the West Coast, but I love the deep poetry of the South too much. Tennessee in April would be gentle and healing. I could almost smell the pines and feel the breeze in my lungs. One more sleepless night in one more hotel room and then back to the southland and my lovely life, back to the sweet old women with those genteel accents that make you feel safe and loved, back to "sweetheart" and "baby" and "yes, sir" and "no, sir" and open spaces, farms and grazing livestock, horses walking slowly beneath the gentle mountains, dogs on front porches, back to the music in my veins. For now, night was closing in on the City of Angels. If it held true to form, no one would sleep in this room tonight. As with the nights before, we were awakened at 10:00 p.m. by that strange cry. It would revisit us again at midnight and 3:00 a.m. and 6:00 a.m. Once again, at 8:00 a.m., we tried to wipe the sand out of our eyes and steel up for the day's events. The hotel-to-airliner ritual of packing, checking out of the room, hugging my sister-in-law good-bye, checking the bags, boarding, and finally settling in the seat went off without a hitch. By now we were doing this in our sleep (literally). Soon, we pushed from the gate, and there was movement, sweet movement. We looked down on our baby girl as the plane achieved speed, then lift, and then wheels were up. Next stop: Nashville and home.

The flight was mercifully half full and quiet for four hours. We breathed in and breathed out. We collected ourselves and pulled it together. There would be a crowd waiting on us back at home. There would be visitors and aunts and uncles and grandparents and well-wishers surrounding us for days. Time to put the trauma of the last three weeks into humorous, easy-to-recite, small, compartmentalized stories and get on with the business of getting on with business. The middle American air space looked fresh and clean. The clouds seemed whiter. The sky was bluer. All of this would be a great dinner story and, who knows, maybe even a good talk show topic. I hadn't thought about the career in weeks. Would this make it more interesting? Less interesting? Would anybody even care? At that moment, I was just exhausted and longing for my own bed. I hadn't slept in a week. I wanted to watch the local news with my feet up on the coffee table. I wanted to be home with my family and watch my little girl blossom into a walking, talking baby whirlwind. I knew the peace and nurturing embrace of home would be all it would take. Once again, this little mystery would continue to confound.

After four mercifully quiet hours in the crisp air, we felt the descent and heard the deadened roar of the landing gear coming down. The green south was getting closer, and soon the wheels touched down. As we taxied to the gate, Yolanda and I were both in full adrenaline rush. The haze of this odyssey was now clearing. Our home and family would now place us on terra firma with our little rag doll. We exited the plane and found a restroom where Yolanda could change Isabella into a little traditional Chinese outfit we purchased in Guangzhou. She returned refreshed and carrying the most gorgeous little china doll I'd ever seen. Isabella had begun shaking and squealing in delight whenever she saw me, even if she'd just seen me two minutes earlier. The elation on the little china doll's face produced a smile on mine that would carry me down the escalator into the bosom of my waiting family. As we descended to the baggage claim area in the BNA airport, thirty to forty family members and friends greeted us with applause, whistles, and signs with Bella's picture on them. We were showered with love and well wishes; the journey was complete (we thought). The China doll was worshipped and adored by new, round-eyed uncles and aunts and cousins and grandparents. She didn't take to it well and began crying. Still, we knew this was just an overload of stimulation and people. We'll get home; all will be well there. We loaded the car and began the final trek to our home with a full caravan of family members behind us.

April in Nashville was every bit as stunning as I'd pictured it in my mind's eye—cloudless and calm, warm and green. It indeed felt like a second chance. The drive to Franklin from the Nashville airport was peaceful and soothing. Isabella had still been crying when we placed her in the new car seat. By the time we were on the interstate, however, James Taylor's "Line 'Em Up" (that just happened to be in the CD player when we left) had calmed her. Little did I know how many times I'd be singing and playing that song for the next two years. It seemed to have a healing effect. We drove, Yolanda looking out one side and me looking out the other. We were quiet and exhausted. The trees and power poles flew by, and the lines on the road were hypnotic. We drove past Briley Parkway to I-440 West, on to I-65, and then south to home. I pulled out my cell phone and called my manager. I had no idea what I was going to be doing for the next few weeks. It was a Friday, April 11. "Hey, Stu, Regie here. I'm back with the little refugee (my management company was called Refugee

Management, and "the little refugee" had been our pet name for Isabella), and we're almost to the house. Any news I should know about?" He hemmed and hawed and asked lots of questions about the trip. I understood this would be a little adventure I'd be recounting for years to come. I hit the high spots: SARS, sick Chinese baby, two trips to the hospital, fourteen hours of screaming on the plane, CDC, etc, etc. It was a good story. I had lived it, and now I was ready to get on with the career. I needed him to say, "I've got more than we can get to on a phone call" or "It's all unbelievable; let me call you when you get home." I needed him to say almost anything other than what he said.

"Well, uh, there's some stuff to cover but not now. Go home. Get over the jet lag. Take as much time as you need. Call me Monday, and we'll dig into it." This didn't sound good.

"We still have a hit song though, right?" I asked off the cuff.

"Uh, maybe yes, maybe no," he said, half-joking.

"What does that mean, Stu?" I retorted in what I'm sure was a worried tone. When I'd left the United States, my single was at number fifteen with a bullet and climbing faster than any other song on the charts. The last thing my booking agent said to me was, "Get ready to work; you're about to be a star." How could all that have changed in three weeks?

"You're scaring me, man. We okay?" I asked pleadingly.

"Just too much to go into right now. Get your sleep worked out. Get some rest. We'll talk Monday. We'll come over and see the baby. I'm glad you guys are home safe. Don't worry. Everything's going to be all right."

It didn't sound all right. Get some rest? Everybody kept telling me to get rest. They obviously didn't know this china doll.

I could see the familiar exit in the distance. At that exit we would turn right at the gas station and then curl for a mile around the access road, past the mini farm on the left and into our subdivision. We would snake around the houses and manicured yards to the small bridge over the creek. The *pa bump, pa bump* sound under the tires would signify that small rise in the road that was the final landmark before turning into our cul-de-sac. Then we'd turn into the second driveway on the right and finally be home.

I'd driven this path thousands of times but never with this much longing. The sweet air of my own living room would be medicine for my weary soul. I pined for the familiar furniture and the creaks in certain places in the floor. I missed my yard and my studio and my bed. As we walked up the three stairs from the garage into the kitchen, I exhaled. A small party was already happening when Yolanda, Isabella, and I walked in. My parents had taken the liberty of providing food and beverages and seeing to it we didn't have to think about too much. It was lovely. As the china doll was passed around from family member to family member and introduced to the world of Southern baby spoiling, I stood on my deck and looked out over the expansive acreage. This would be a lovely place to raise this child. I could see the swing set and dollhouse. The princess would have whatever she wanted. She already had me wrapped around her precious little finger. I'd only had her a week, but she was already a daddy's girl. This career of mine had gone from a personal quest to a primal instinct. I had to take care of this family. All the lofty, pretentious goals had melted into one overriding theme: provide. The brief conversation with Stu had rattled me, and as I recounted the China story to family members into the night, inside I was panicked. We needed to get the sleeping thing figured out, and then I had to get to work. We had spent a lot of the *American Dreams* advance money paying for the adoption (around 20,000 dollars), and although we weren't broke, I was looking ahead. I'd taken a big risk; now there was a child in the balance.

One by one, the family disbursed. Kisses and pats and baby talk and generally all manner of doting that can be done was done to this little china doll. She would be loved beyond measure; that much was true. "Once she gets in a good routine and figures out the time change, she's going to be just fine" was the prevailing wisdom of the mothers and grandmothers as they rubbed her little head and walked out the door. We were hoping. Darkness was falling. Would tonight be the night? Would the rag doll sleep one night all the way through? At some point she would have to, we thought. This was about routine and good nutrition. We had plenty of friends who'd adopted children internationally. It wasn't abnormal for some kids to take a few weeks to stabilize. We might have a few bad days ahead, maybe not. Maybe we'd get lucky. As bedtime came around, Yolanda crawled in the tub and bathed the rag doll. We powdered and changed and fed the night-night bottle. There was soft music and dim lights in the room.

It was sure making me sleepy. Hopefully it would make her sleepy too. We gently placed her for the first time in the expensive, new crib, with fresh, new blankets around her. The room wasn't too warm or too chilled. These were perfect baby sleeping conditions. Sleep, little rag doll. Sleep for hours and hours. Mommy and Daddy are tired.

"Good night, princess; you're home for good."

At 10:00 p.m. the screaming started.

"Dude, really?" Yolanda said, wiping her eyes.

"What do we do?" I asked, my creaky voice cutting in and out. "Do we let her cry it out? She doesn't need a bottle; you think she needs to be changed?" I was mumbling and running through the new parent lexicon.

"Oh, Regie, I don't know. I just want to sleep!" said Yolanda in an injured tone. "Why won't she sleeeeeep?" As long as the whine was happening, there was no sleep in the house. I broke.

"I'll get up and walk her. You try to sleep; we'll do this in shifts if we have to." I put on my sweats, stumbled to her room, and picked up the little bundle. "Okay, sweetie, Daddy's got you," I said in the baby talk voice. "I know this is all strange and new to you, but you gotta learn how to sweepies," I whispered while pacing her room and patting her tiny bum. She wouldn't collapse on my shoulder like I'd seen kids do before. She fidgeted and lunged backward and fell from side to side. This had been happening for a week, but in China I guess I didn't notice as much. Now, in the solemn scrutiny of her room, I watched her closely. Was there something wrong with her? Surely not. "Come on, baby girl. Lay your head on Daddy's shoulder." She pushed away and continued to wobble. My rag doll was not sleeping, not clinging, not sitting up, not crawling. Every so often, she would go into a screaming fit. I knew this would keep Yolanda awake and disturbed, so at midnight, I decided to take the first of what would be hundreds of moonlit drives. "Let's go listen to James," I whispered to her as we snuck down the stairs. I was up now. I figured Yolanda should sleep as long as she could, so I took the baby into the garage and placed her in the baby seat. The garage door was raised, JT was in, and we were out of the driveway and into the night. We'd drive as long as I could hold out. The *Hourglass* CD opens with the opening line of the song, "I remember Richard Nixon back in..." JT crooned; Isabella squealed. All was well for at least three and half minutes. Out of the subdivision onto the main highway, onto the interstate. "Line 'em, up, line 'em all up." He glided out of the car speakers. My rag doll was happy and quiet. Maybe she would sleep in the car, and we could make a smooth transition into the crib. With the opening strains of track two, the crying started again. I feverishly hit the button that took us to track one. "I remember Richard Nixon back in ... " brought squeals of delight. It appeared we would be listening to "Line 'Em Up" all night. By 1:00 a.m., we'd played it seven times. Here we went into the second hour. "I remember Richard ... " brought the squeals again. James, Bella, and I had a long night ahead of us. By 4:00 a.m., I was spent, and I was sure Isabella was too. Maybe the night drive had calmed her down enough to sleep for few hours. After all, we were trying to gradually acclimate to the new time zone. We'd been in so many over the past three days, I was sure she would level out. This had to simply be a temporary situation. Other parents had stories of their kids not sleeping when they were babies. Come on; babies are weird. Isabella would get in a groove; I had to believe that. As I walked back up the stairs with the mysterious bundle, I could see the sun sneaking up on us through the windows. Like vampires running from sunlight, we hurried up the stairs into her darkened room. She was calm. She was quiet. Surely, she'd sleep now, maybe a few hours. Bundled down in the crib with baby blankets around her, she smiled at me. I walked away thinking success had been achieved. My sweats and socks were off, and I was finally under the covers, my body jerking and twitching from fatigue. Suddenly, the screams began. Yolanda woke with a start.

"Oh, how long did she sleep?"

I replied in disbelief, "She didn't. I've been driving around all night listening to 'Line 'Em Up.' I'm spent. I really can't do it anymore. Can you take over?"

"I got it," she said, dressing and huffing and puffing from the startling scream. I drifted off, and Yolanda took the morning shift. This had to be severe jet lag; we could push through it. We were fit and up for it. It might last a couple of more nights or maybe even a coupe of more weeks, but we were sure we could do it.

It went on like that for days. Somewhere, I started losing track of everything. By Monday, I was hazy and not together, but I had business to accomplish. What was happening with this song? Where was my career? What was next? I called Stuart, and we set up the meeting. I collected myself and drove into town. By the time I was in the elevator to the forth floor offices, I was collected and back to business.

"Okay, guys. What's going on?" I was focused. Norb (my day-to-day guy and radio guru) spoke up and gave me the condensed version. "We lost the single, man, just that simple. It was rocking, and then the label had a merger with another label, and you just got steamrolled by some other acts from the imprint they just bought. We think we had some bad testing somewhere as well, and it might've turned 'em cold on it. I can't confirm that, but that's what I think. I still think we can salvage this. You gotta do as many shows as you can. We gotta sell CDs at the shows and report them. If the label sees more movement, maybe they'll kick things up a notch."

"Let me get this straight. We brought the record. We brought Delilah in. We basically did all of it, and now we have to do more?"

"Yep. That's the way it works," he said bluntly.

"All right. I now have an insomniac baby to feed. Let's go to work."

William Morris had booked me on some one-off dates that required a band. The dates didn't pay enough to cover the band, so I'd be going in the hole for those. Ah, the glamour of rock and roll. I was looking forward to any date I could get out of town. I just wanted a quiet hotel room where I could sleep for eight hours, nothing more.

Back at the house, Yolanda was working with the little rag doll, trying to get her to stand or sit up or hold her head straight.

It wasn't working. By the time I got back home, Yolanda had cataloged everything she was doing or not doing and was observing every little detail and movement. Momma was on the case.

"Reg, I think something might be wrong with this baby. We need to get her to a doctor immediately, but I also think we might need to talk to some specialists," she said in that urgent tone that always kind of unsettles me. We knew we would have to go to the doctor anyway, so we made that appointment right then. That single doctor visit would change the course of our lives. It would wreck our future and change the trajectory of every part of our motion. One random phone call to one random doctor would color everything from that moment to this. The doctor came highly recommended. He had seen hundreds of little girls newly adopted from China and was on the waiting list for one of his own. So we picked up the phone and made the appointment. This was a good thing, we thought. Maybe he could share some insight on our situation. Maybe there was some magical thing we would learn as new parents that would set our feet on solid ground with this little girl. Maybe after this visit she would sleep; we just needed sleep.

While waiting on the fateful doctor appointment, we slogged through night after sleepless night. We customized chairs and baby walkers to prop up the rag doll so she could watch *Sesame Street* and every other children's show known to man. This little girl had been obsessed with TV since her fever broke in Guangzhou. We weren't sure if it was because she'd never seen TV or because that's all she was exposed to in her foster home. We knew she'd been strapped in a crib. Did they just place her in front of the TV for hours at a time? There was no way of knowing, but her obsession with the tube was real, and it calmed her. We were more than willing to use it. By the second week at home, we were already breaking and placing her in front of the TV long enough to lay next to her on the couch and rest for twenty minutes. We swore we'd never be *those* parents, but here we were allowing Cookie Monster to raise our child. Two weeks without full sleep will make you do things you swore you wouldn't. We were trying to survive. Our family and friends (with children) seemed to take sick pleasure in our exhaustion. We had been the couple everyone envied—plenty of money, no children, exciting travel schedule, movies every weekend, fully rested all the time. They were secretly enjoying the fact that we had a nonsleeper on our hands, and they all knew she'd eventually come around. This little wrinkle seemed like just irony, I'm sure. Inside the walls of our house, however, we knew in our hearts something was wrong. After two weeks, with great nutrition and as much routine as could be accomplished, clean sheets, clean air, and more love than can be showered on one individual, the baby still wouldn't sit up. She still wasn't trying to stand or mimic speech or grab anything with her fingers. She was clearly delayed in some way. As badly as we needed sleep, we needed answers even more. The chuckles on the other ends phone lines and the obligatory "she'll come around" from family and friends were starting to wear thin. The rag doll was a mystery that was not unraveling. What was wrong with my little girl?

The realities of money were bearing down as well. I'd been doing shows and covering the band's pay out of my pocket. The gigs I was getting weren't paying well enough yet, and now that my single had died, the crowds weren't showing up. Birmingham, Chattanooga, Knoxville, regional shows that were booked when I was hitting were moderate successes. I could feel myself waning on stage as well. By the second month Isabella was home, my exhaustion level was at a place I didn't know existed. Getting out of a chair was work. After the show in Birmingham, I drove through the night to Atlanta to do a CNN Father's Day piece.

The story of the adoption had hit some of the press and the man-who-writes-baby-song-brings-home-Chinese-orphan angle was warm and fuzzy and ripe for Father's Day. I'd slept two hours in the hotel room in Atlanta and was in the makeup chair at seven. Some famous CNN female anchor was chain smoking and hitting on me from the next chair. I couldn't focus. "Too bad you're married, sweetheart," she said in that eerie news voice. *Man, is this some weird dream or am I really awake?* I thought to myself. *She just reported on a congressional budget deal and the Iraq war. Now she's puffing on Marlboros and hitting on me? This is surreal.* My thoughts were clouded. I was slow to answer questions. I had to think hard to remember what had just been asked. My usual quick wit and wry quips (a gift inherited from my father) were conspicuously absent. I felt heavy, and my eyes were puffy. I could barely get through the interview. As the red light illuminated and cameras rolled, the dimwitted (and clearly frustrated to be doing this puff piece on me) Barbie doll CNN correspondent lunged into her intro.

"Well, the man who brought the world 'Butterfly Kisses' is back with a new take on family and fatherhood. I'm here today with Regie Hamm. Regie—" I stopped her midsentence. "Actually, I didn't bring 'Butterfly Kisses' to anyone. My friend Bob Carlisle did. But I did work on that record, and I sure do love Bob and that song." All the perfectly coiffed news anchors in the studio were staring blankly at me. I threw her off her game. "Okay, well, (looking at her notes) you did work on that song, and it clearly affected you. Let's talk about your hit 'Babies' and this very special Father's Day you'll be having."

What was I doing? I wasn't flowing like I should've been. I called out an entertainment reporter during a live worldwide feed. Was I insane? I couldn't get it together. I couldn't smile; it hurt to smile. I couldn't answer the questions quickly. I rambled and mumbled and couldn't get my mouth to say what I was thinking. What *was* I thinking? My brows furrowed. I suddenly looked like a politician caught in a lie. "This is a feel-good piece, Regie. Smile, you idiot!" my inner coach kept screaming. I couldn't smile or unfurrow the brows. My body would not respond to its commands. Minute after excruciating minute passed. I can't remember what I said or did, but mercifully, the five-minute piece ended, and I was done. I shook hands with the Barbie doll and waved to the crew and talking heads as I exited, trying to appear as cool and unaffected as possible. Just like that, my close-up was finished. I wiped the pancake makeup off, changed into driving clothes, and headed north, back to Nashville, the rag doll, and the mystery.

The visit was as mundane and ordinary as any other doctor visit. It was your garden variety, post-China extraction, baby checkup. By the time we were in the waiting room, we knew all was not right with our child's brain. We knew all was not right with her body. We were hoping for answers. "Isabella Hamm" rang out in the waiting room. It would only be the first of thousands of times I would hear that cadence. We walked back to the doctor's office, stopping along the way to get readings of weight, length, temperature, and blood pressure. The doctor entered and began his routine. He quietly and nimbly bent, squeezed, turned, listened, looked, felt, and inspected. "Okay," he said under his breath. "Hmm. Okay," he said again under his breath. Yolanda and I watched and waited like game show contestants wondering what we'd won. He scratched something on a chart and then said, "Well, she's got some movement issues but nothing out of the ordinary for a newly adopted child from China. Many of these little tics you're seeing will go away in time. It can take months to work all of the trauma and confusion out. How's she sleeping?"

We looked at each other. "She hasn't slept a full night yet," Yolanda said.

"Okay, Mom and Dad, you're going to have to have some tough love here. For the next two weeks, you're just going to have to let her cry it out. I know it's painful and it feels cruel, but if you don't let her figure out how to sleep on her own, she never will."

We looked at each other again. Parents know when something's deeper than normal. We knew in our collective gut that wasn't all there was to it, but we smiled and said, "Okay, we just needed assurance we weren't being horrible parents."

"No, no. It's a common thing for rookies. By the time you're on your third, you'll be pros," he said with a chuckle. "Okay, let's get her caught up on her shots. I'm ordering a full round. We'll re-immunize her for what she got in China just to be sure. She'll be all caught up today." Yolanda and I looked at each other again, this time with concern. The thing about health Nazis is they read too much. We knew about the ongoing controversy with immunizations and autism. We were against immunizing in bulk at the very least. The mercury (immunizations sometimes carry a mercury based substance called Thymerosol that has been allegedly linked to autism) issue is one thing, but this guy was about to inject this nine-month-old baby with forty-three diseases. When I was a kid, I got eight shots. Today, kids are immunized on a grand scale. I'm not here to argue for or against it. I am not a doctor, but I do wonder if that many immunizations at once are good for the developing child—my own opinion, nothing more.

I spoke up. "Um, we've decided not to get the immunizations today. We're going to wait a while on that."

He lowered his head and removed his glasses. "Don't tell me you're some of those. Please don't tell me that. All of this baloney about mercury and autism is just crap. It's all been debunked.

Immunizations are being done for the sake of children's health," he roared, visibly upset.

"I just think we'd at least like to space these things out; I don't personally believe the issue has been settled to our satisfaction. These are our wishes," I said in the most humble and contrite way I could.

"If you're not immunizing, then I'm not your doctor. Period. I don't have time for this nonsense. I read the medical journals. Do you think I would do this to my own children if I thought it was unsafe? You're spending too much time on conspiracy Web sites. I'm talking about science, not science fiction." His voice was raising now.

"Sir, I just think something is causing all these autism cases. I'm making no judgment other than reserving the right to choose when and how many immunizations my daughter will receive," I said, my voice starting to rise.

"Fine with me, but I'm not your doctor. Get out of my office. If you decide to change your mind, I'll be here. If not, please don't come back. See the payment and insurance person on the way out," he said tersely. My blood was boiling. I'm sure his was too. We'd fallen squarely in the middle of a raging philosophical debate. We traded the detachment and slip-shod, assembly-line practices of communist health care for the deep tectonic rifts of the American medical landscape. This would not be over soon. It would deepen, broaden, and evolve into a maze of impossibilities I could've never fathomed.

In the midst of shootouts with doctors and fuzzyheaded gigs, Isabella was being reviewed, inspected, and analyzed by every specialist we could find. Several therapists from the Tennessee Early Intervention Services program had been by our house to look at her. At almost ten months, she was still behaving like a newborn. Two months home should've solved many of these issues. Upon unanimous recommendations, we filed reams and reams of paperwork and applied for therapies through the state. She would get speech, occupational, and physical therapy three days a week. I've seen the worst of government run programs, but I was very thankful for this one. Every day, we learned about what Bella could and couldn't do. As the onion was peeled, it became more and more heartbreaking. As she closed in on her first birthday, she couldn't perform the basic pincher grasp, which is normally mastered by around six months old and is the cornerstone of all human civilization. If you think about it, without being able to grasp something between your thumb and index finger, nothing else in our organized society would be possible. It's a movement that is taken so completely for granted; we never think about its importance. Raising a child without that ability is maddening.

The summer was hell. It had now been months since anyone in my house had slept a full night. We were already operating in shifts, a practice that would continue for years to come. My parents and other friends would come help, but there was nothing much anyone could really do. It was clear that my daughter was severely, mentally delayed. She was also some sort of otherworldly insomniac. One night in the throes of sleep deprivation, I stared at her while futilely trying rock her to sleep. I stared at her face closely. Suddenly her almond shaped eyes sparked some deep, dark memory of the aliens I'd seen on TV as a kid. They called them the grays. I had been an *X-Files* fan. It all made sense now. She was an alien! That's the only way it could be explained. How can a child survive without sleep? This had to be the explanation! Suddenly, she cooed, and I returned to my senses. That little mental wormhole would be repeated many times over the following years. This was just the beginning of the long, slow descent into a dark world of mental confusion brought on by sleep deprivation.

The money I had saved was gone. The gigs weren't coming. The label was committed to testing a single in the Triple A format, but "Babies" had officially been dropped. My one chance to resurrect it was a show with Delilah in Knoxville. There were supposed to be twenty-five hundred rabid Delilah fans there. They would know the song. Three hundred *American Dreams* CDs were to be drop shipped to the venue by the label. If we could sell at least a hundred CDs or so, it would show up as a spike in sales, and they would re-think the single. As it turned out, a tornado in Knoxville kept most of the people home. The CDs were sent to the wrong location, and I had no product to sell. Even with the diminished crowd, I could've easily sold a hundred CDs at that show, but they were locked up in an office across town. These are the subtle (random) misses that make or break a life or career. These are the details that keep you awake at night five years later when you're wondering how it all fell apart. Everything that could go wrong did. In six short months, I'd gone from the golden boy who could do no wrong to that guy with the bad luck who ended up painting houses. What was happening? I'd always assumed God would punish me for having a successful career and nice life one day. I just didn't think he'd drag my daughter into it. I needed these details to work. I needed everything to line up. The money that had flowed so freely for so many years was now depleted and wasn't being replenished. I couldn't focus. I needed sleep. I couldn't get a handle on what was happening to me. While that small but profound miss was happening in Knoxville, another one was brewing back at home.

"Reg, the therapists all agreed on something today," Yolanda said in that urgent tone. "They said they couldn't be sure if Isabella would actually ever walk. Even if she does, they think it will require mechanical assistance. Go find me a flat house." The weight of what we were being told was not fully falling on us. By that time we were so embroiled in making it through the day, we didn't focus on years from now. We had to figure out the now. Period. I immediately went to work looking for a house that was handicapped friendly. I had loved my home, purchased on the backs of the songs I'd written, but I loved my daughter more. The house meant nothing to me now. It was a hindrance. The seventeen-step staircase couldn't be navigated by my struggling rag doll. It was getting harder for my wife and I to navigate it with her as well. We needed something flat and practical. We started looking for ranch houses. Every evening, we would strap Isabella in the car seat and drive around Nashville neighborhoods looking for something that looked right while JT lined 'em all up. Day after day, night after night, we scoured the Williamson country area. We didn't want to move too far from our existing house—we didn't have the time or energy for that—and we needed to stay in this county that provided so many services to our special needs daughter. This wasn't vanity or luxury; this was necessity and real life.

As the summer came to a close, we started noticing strange little tics in Isabella, things we'd never seen before.

"Regie, is she having a seizure?" Yolanda asked.

"Nah, I think this is just one of those little things she does," I replied with that fatherly, everything's-going-to-be-okay tone. I remember the night vividly. The sun was sinking behind the French doors that overlooked the backyard. The house was quiet, summery warm, and still. Yolanda and I were in the floor with the baby, kissing on her and trying yet again to get her to sit or stand or pick up a Cheerio. Her face began pulling to one side. We lay on the floor for an hour watching her go in out of these episodes. We stared silently.

"See, Reg, what is that?"

"I think it's just a little facial tic, isn't it? What does a seizure look like? I've never seen anybody have one. Do they look like this?"

Yolanda stared. "See, there she goes again. I think she's having seizures. Is that a seizure?"

More confused, I asked, "What do we do if it is one? Do we go to the emergency room? Do we call somebody? This is something I've never dealt with. I don't know what to do." Just then, she stopped and smiled. We looked at each other in bewilderment.

"I don't know, Reg. That was weird, and I'm a little worried."

I was too. I was worried about a lot of things. Just when I thought the bottom would fall out of our lives completely, a call from an old friend saved the summer. Shawn McSpadden, my first publisher and now head of Word Records, had heard through my good friend and one-time manager, Brian Boland, that I might be back on the production market, so he called about me producing a project. Random. It would be easy work. It was for Gaither Vocal Band vocal virtuoso, David Phelps. He was a world-class, well-established singer with a built-in audience. There would be no new ground to break here. I just had to find or write great songs, record him well, and collect my card production rate. This was a layup and something I simply had to have to stay afloat. I was loath to step back into the world of Christian music, but I had no choice. It was either this or nothing. Nothing wasn't an option, so I began the painstaking process I had begun so many times before of writing songs for someone else, finding songs for someone else, booking musicians, booking studios, coordinating schedules, meetings with the label and artist, finding the direction and sound, delivering on time and under budget. Shawn had saved my summer whether he knew it or not. I was dealing with an artist career on the brink of disaster, a special needs child, and finding and purchasing a new house. My stress level was higher than it had ever been. There were no grandiose thoughts anymore. Pip had never found himself in this position. In fact, that was just a classic novel written over a hundred years ago; it was fiction. I was living in the real world now. The pontificating and strategizing and philosophical navel gazing had stopped. I needed money. I could produce. Where do I sign? I was making yet another small surrender.

WELCOME TO HOLLYWOOD

I'd done this thousands of times before, but now something was different. I lost an edge somewhere. I'd spent two months producing this record. I thought it had gone well. We came in under budget and on time, and I had handed them a first single that would go on to be a chart topper. I was doing all I had ever done, but I knew I had lost a step. The endless months of sleep deprivation were wearing on me in new and interesting ways. My live shows had lost luster. Now, the years of chiseled bedrock that was my craft—the understanding of songs and record making—was eroding as well. My attention span was shortening. My fatigue level was so high I could barely sit through a vocal session. Songwriting seemed like a silly process that ultimately produced nothing intrinsic. My once focused, laser-sharp processor was slow and distracted.

The record I made that summer was the best I could muster, but ultimately it fell short of my expectations and, I think, everyone else's. This was just survival, and I wasn't used to it. I was used to winning on a grand scale, knocking it out of the park, not just settling for a base hit. This was a base hit. The musicians were great. The singer was great. The producer was uninspired and impaired and wouldn't be sparking a lot of interest in further projects from anyone. It doesn't take long for people to get a sense of trouble surrounding particular talent. There was a sense of trouble all around me, and no one wanted any part of it. Shawn had handed this to me as a gift, but no one would be able to do that twice, and I knew it. This would be the last production call I ever got from a record label in Christian music. That part of my life was now over and not on my own terms. The little girl I had brought home from Asia was becoming my undoing, and it was just the beginning.

I had one last shot at dazzling my record label: a show at the House of Blues in Chicago, opening for the Neville Brothers. It was sold out, and the song "Infidels" was number one on the Triple A radio station there. On September 5, I would walk out on that stage in front of four thousand Neville Brothers fans and literally play for my life. While waiting to do that show, I found a house in Nashville, a one-story ranch built in 1973 by a widow, who still lived there, and not touched since. It was about as bad as any house needing renovations can be—orange shag carpet, avocado appliances, dark paneling, popcorn ceilings, landscaping out of control and growing into the foundation, one HVAC unit not working, no easy access to the front door; the list goes on and on. But it was in a good neighborhood in Williamson County. It was one level with a long, easy hallway to navigate, and the price was right. I looked at the place seven times before finally bringing Yolanda to see it. I walked her through the seventies relic room by room and explained what could be torn out or moved or rebuilt or repainted. We could customize this house for our little one to our own liking. I was thinking she would balk, but she just looked at me bluntly and said, "Buy it."

We put our beautiful home on the market and began the stressful process of selling a house, buying a house, and renovating a house. I would play in Chicago and then come home to close on the seventies ranch house the next week. Maybe this show would jolt the label heads back into "Regie Hamm fever." Maybe a career could be salvaged out of this. Maybe this house was the new beginning I needed. Maybe, maybe, maybe. I had stopped staying in hotels after shows and instead started driving all night back home because I knew Yolanda would need to be relieved in the watching of Isabella. It was tedious, fatiguing work, and it definitely took two people and usually the better part of twenty-four hours a day. Isabella simply didn't sleep. The plan was I would drive to Chi-town, do my thing, and drive back. Eighteen hours round trip. Believe it or not, because of the state I was in mentally, that didn't seem like a problem. My long-time friend and co-writer of the Avalon hit "The Glory," Jim Cooper, offered to drive up with me and help drive back. So we drove north. Being away from Isabella for just a few hours made me exhale and relax. Jim drove, and I stared out the window. Louisville, Indianapolis, Chicago. Friday night traffic was in full force. I had no tension; I had nothing else to do and nowhere else to be until 7:00 p.m. Forty-five minutes after that, I'd have another bite at a career or not. There it was: House of Blues, national treasure, pop music icon, my final shot. We found the loading dock and brought in my Yamaha S-80 (Bertha), the same S-80 that had accompanied me out of the Christian music business and into the clubs of Nashville, the same S-80 that had amazed the radio programmer in Seattle, the same S-80 that had gotten me a record deal with Universal Records. Tonight, we would rely on each other one more time. I sat up at the edge of the large, semicircular stage and looked back at the endless amount of gear that would be the headliner ammunition. It would just be me—no band, no lights, no pyrotechnics—just me, a kid from Nashville on a piano, trying to win the hearts and minds of four thousand people in one of Americas hottest venues. No pressure.

A white boy walking out on a stage facing thousands of Neville Brothers fans is the stuff of which nightmares are made. I might as well have been in my underwear playing for my senior class. I never get nervous on stage. I've been on stage my whole life; it's my home. This night, I was downright terrified. I sat down at the keyboard while they coughed and cleared their throats and stared at me. I adjusted myself, looked them in the eyes, and began. First song—moderate applause. Second song—I picked up a few fans. Third song—I almost had them. The Elton John medley was next; that always works. The true story of listening to Elton John records in the basement of a church while my father was presiding over a church service above me is a crowd pleaser. I knew if this one didn't work, nothing would. First transition into "Bennie and the Jets"—applause, laughter—I had them. For a brief moment, I was back on my game. They were laughing, singing, and applauding at the right times. This was good. Then when I was done, something strange happened. A group of over-served ladies in the front row started yelling out classic piano songs from the seventies and eighties. I went with it—"Feeling Alright" into Journey's "Faithfully" into the hypnotic "Walking in Memphis." Finally, the obligatory yell: "Play 'Piano Man!'" ("Freebird" for piano players.) It was one of my all time greatest fears, and it was happening at the House of Blues in Chicago. People were yelling requests I hadn't practiced. Somehow though, my instincts kicked in, and I was balanced on the head of a pin for about twenty minutes, adrenalin in full explosion. I was dead on with every song. Keys and progressions just came to me. This was working. I was certain I was winning the night. As I crooned the final, "You got us feeling all right" of every ivory tickler's most enduring cliché,

"Piano Man," I jumped right into my local hit, "Infidels." By the end of it, I had made the crowd laugh and sing and applaud, standing O. Maybe I was back. Maybe this night had turned it around. We needed this—not just me anymore—*we* needed it as a family. "Thank you, Chicago. Good night!" I bowed, patted Bertha, and the lights went down. I packed up and walked past Aaron Neville as he entered the stage. We exchanged nods, and I rolled my cherished Bertha back to the van. I collected my five hundred dollars while the Zydeco funk chugged into motion, changed into driving clothes in the green room, and was headed south before the Neville Brothers were into their fourth song. There was no radio meet and greet or hotel room trashing. No chilling at a bar or watching the headliner. I had a little mystery to get back to. Hopefully this night would help me keep her fed for another year.

Back at home life had gone into full-scale chaos trying to sell our house and purchase the new relic. We would spend the month packing and taking trips to Goodwill and fixing all those little things on a house you never fix until you sell it. In the middle of this madness, Isabella had her first grand mal seizure at home. This time, Yolanda and I didn't watch her and pontificate. We loaded her up and went to the Vanderbilt emergency room. Her fever was spiking, and she wasn't coming out of the seizure. We rushed into the emergency room gingerly holding the little bundle who'd seen too many hospitals already. Forms were signed; vitals were taken; she was taken from us and quickly rushed into a room. They had to bring her out of the seizure. It was like a scene from *ER*—young residents running here and there yelling phrases with "stat" at the end of them. The next time I saw my baby, she was in a room surrounded by ten people talking to each other in disturbingly serious tones. The IV was in the arm (thank God, the arm); electrodes were monitoring her; finally, she settled.

"You want to hold her, Mom?" One of the nurses nodded to Yolanda after she was stabilized.

"Of course," Yolanda quickly replied. My little one-year-old was now out of it and bobbing her head around with droopy eyes. Just when we thought she was out of the woods, she locked a gaze on to Yolanda and froze. "Bella, baby, Bella, Bella." Her voice getting higher and more panicked. Isabella wasn't responding. She was locked in a seizure and had begun twitching and jerking. I looked at the clock. It had been three minutes, and Yolanda was starting to lose it. "Bella, baby, Bella, baby! Come on, sweetie. It's Mommy! Regie, she's not responding! Do something, do something!" The nurses were gathered around her checking vitals and trying different things. Five minutes…still seizing. My heart was beating out of my chest now. My mouth was producing too much saliva, and I couldn't get a handle on my thoughts. I tried to appear calm for Yolanda.

"It's okay, Landa. She'll be okay." I didn't believe it; I thought we would lose her then and there. Six minutes and still seizing. At this point, the professionals were panicking. Now I was scared. They grabbed Isabella out of Yolanda's arms, and a nurse tried to usher us out the door. "Mr. and Mrs. Hamm, we need to work on her. Follow me, please," she said in the most professional voice she could muster.

"I'm not going anywhere while my daughter is seizing like that!" Yolanda screamed, now being physically restrained. "Do something! Please do something!" Yolanda was screaming through hysterical tears. I looked at the clock. Seven minutes and still seizing. I was palpitating and praying, "No, no, no" under my breath. The room started to spin. This was the most helpless feeling I'd ever experienced in my life. I couldn't help her. I couldn't protect her. Her little eyes were locked in a gaze, and I feared that would be the last time I would see them. Shifting into high gear, the doctors and nurses wheeled Isabella out of the room down the hall to someplace else. They were in life-saving mode now.

Thirty minutes later, a man in a white coat and blue smock walked up to us calmly with a half smile that was reassuring. "She came out of the seizure fine, but we're keeping her overnight for observation." We both exhaled.

"Oh, thank God." Yolanda breathed, collapsing into me.

"Why is she seizing?" I asked.

"We think it's all related to her fever. Some kids do this. I really think she'll be fine now."

Yolanda and I were pros in the business of Bella care by now. "I'll take care of her for now. Why don't you run home and get us some fresh clothes and pack up a food bag?" I knew exactly what food to bring. I also knew which clothes. Bella's care had become a full-time job and one in which we were both intimately involved. Thirty minutes home, thirty minutes to pack, thirty minutes back. Another long, uncomfortable night was ahead.

Even under a constant drip of heavy sedation, Isabella would wake up every few hours and look around. How was she doing this? I was amazed by her sheer capacity to live without sleep. Something deeper had to be going on with this kid. I'd never heard of this kind of insomnia before. The doctors were actually amazed as well. They decided to do a brain scan on her while she was there to see if there was some sort of damage that would explain her delays and sleep patterns. We were eager to get that done. In a strange way, we were secretly hoping they would find something. The absolute darkness we were in was maddening. How do you treat something when you have no idea what it is? If she had brain damage, we would at least know and be able to start gearing her therapy toward that problem. It would be a start.

They came and wheeled her down around 6:00 a.m. We'd kept her up for a few hours in hopes that she would sleep long enough to get the scan done. Thankfully, it worked. She fell out taking a bottle and was out just long enough for all manner of electrodes to be taped to her tiny head. Scan after scan, wave after wave, minute after minute in the sterile, dimly lit room with one rocking chair—it was another all-nighter. Hopefully, this one would produce answers.

The tests were done, and the baby was irritable and crying. We signed the insurance forms and release papers while we were packing her up. We stepped into the stark, cool sunlight, strapped ourselves in the car, and made the thirty-minute trek back to Franklin. Now we would wait for results and pray with all we had that Isabella didn't go into any more seizures. She would have to be monitored closely all the time now. This was a new wrinkle in this incredibly difficult saga. I knew in my heart that being on the road would be out of the question. As it turns out, it wouldn't matter. The China/SARS ordeal had ignited some mild interest for a documentary on us, maybe even an Oprah show, but as all things related to pop culture (and unfortunately, in this country, big epidemics fall into that category), once it was off the front page of the news and only a few hundred people in China had died, it wasn't pitchable anymore. The Chicago show had been a success, but not enough of one to make a difference with the bean counters in New York. I was suddenly deemed too invisible to throw large sums of money at again. I flew to LA to meet with my agent out there. It was a last-ditch effort at drumming up gigs anywhere. I thought a face-to-face visit might evoke a little sympathy and make him throw me a bone or two. As I was pleading my case, a very high-profile manager walked in his office, interrupted our meeting, and started talking about the good old days with Sinatra and Sammy. As I listened and laughed in the right places, they joked about fees and star power—things I knew I could not offer them. I knew then and there I was in over my head, and there was no way this guy was giving me a second thought once I walked out the door. This was over. I flew home in defeat, another small surrender. Just as I was learning that my daughter was prone to seizures, just as I was selling my dream house and buying a fixer-upper, just as I was coming to the realization that I wasn't going to be called to produce anymore records, I was informed via e-mail that my CD, *American Dreams*, the CD that the head of my label had said (a mere six months earlier) was his favorite record of the last twenty years and maybe some of the best lyric writing he'd ever heard, the CD that was destined to succeed, would be effectively dropped from the Universal roster, and they weren't giving it back to me; they just weren't spending any more money on it or me as an artist. They also weren't pressing any more copies for release or sale. Basically, I was dropped, and I couldn't have my master back to shop anywhere else. It's the cruelest music business way of telling you, "You're done." In January I was the hottest thing on the charts and the toast of the town. By October I couldn't get my phone calls returned and had no idea how I was going to make a living. I remember wondering, *Can it get worse?* I was about to learn it can always get worse.

AND IT'S A LONG WAY DOWN

*Y*olanda, what are all these medical bills?" I asked. "This looks like the insurance company didn't cover any of Isabella's hospital stay. They're saying we owe like fifteen thousand dollars here. Is this right?" I asked in a concerned tone. We still had some investments that could be cashed in, but once we did that, we'd be in full panic mode. I was sure that wouldn't happen.

"Honey, they sometimes do that. We just have to refile with them. No big deal." She always took care of that stuff, and it made me feel better to talk to her about it. So we refiled. No big deal. But the bills kept coming back.

"Man, I'm going to have to spend a whole day with these guys on the phone clearing this thing up! I hate insurance companies sometimes!" Yolanda barked in that hot, Latin, angry tone you never want to hear. "Let me do this right now before I forget," she huffed. Yolanda doesn't procrastinate. Before I could sufficiently read the documents, she had someone from the insurance company on the phone. I could hear her going through the formalities of names, account numbers, and social security numbers. I then heard her tone change. Oh no.

"What? You're kidding! Why? Can you tell me what it said? There has to be a mistake here...this is...but...in our policy. Really? But...no, no, no, we had...for years now...how? Hold on. Talk to my husband." She was physically shaking, and tears were welling up in her eyes. "Reg, I can't believe this. Talk to this woman. This can't be happening." Her voice was cracking.

"Hi, this is Regie Hamm. Who is this?" I threw my most serious ready-for-business tone. Eight months ago, saying, "This is Regie Hamm" on the phone meant something to people. It clearly meant nothing to the deadpan robot at the other end of this line.

"Sir, I was explaining to your wife that your daughter has been dropped from your insurance policy." Her voice was official and emotionless. She sounded middle-aged, clearly Southern, and possibly African American. She'd obviously made this call before and had learned the art of cold detachment. I could almost feel her reading a magazine and doing her nails while I pleaded my case.

"But she's our child. How can she just be dropped like this? What's the reason?" I pleaded.

"Sir, on her last doctor visit, a preexisting condition was written on her chart by the doctor giving the physical. According to our records, she was adopted at eight months. Your policy clearly states that any child adopted any time after the first twenty-four hours of their birth is subject to policy approval. This preexisting condition has automatically kicked her out of the system. My hands are tied, sir. It's in the policy."

"In the policy? Where in the policy? No one ever told us that. You mean because I adopted my daughter at eight months instead of the day she was born, she's not automatically on my plan?"

"That's correct, sir."

"Doesn't that sound kind of wrong to you? You're punishing this little girl because I couldn't adopt her fast enough?"

"Sir, I don't make the policies, and I didn't sell you yours. You signed the document. We have your signature on file accepting the terms. I may or may not believe it to be wrong, but it's your policy. I'm just the messenger, sir."

"What was on the chart? What is this preexisting condition the doctor wrote down?"

"Let's see. I'm looking at the file now. Hmm," she said under breath. "I'm sorry, sir, by law, I'm not allowed to discuss it with you. Only the patient."

"You're kidding, right? The patient is a thirteen-month-old child. Would you like to speak to her? You seriously can't tell me what's on this chart? I have to fix this. This little girl simply cannot go uninsured! You have no idea what you're doing to my life here. Is there any code that can be typed in to make this go away? Is there a workaround we can find? Can I pay a higher premium? Can we rewrite the policy? Do you have *any* solutions for me? I'm willing to do whatever it takes! Ma'am, I'm begging you. I'm at your mercy here. You have no idea what's happened to my family in the last six months. Please help us work this out! Please!" There was silence on the other end. It sounded for a moment like she was shuffling paper and checking options. Maybe I'd appealed to her common decency. Maybe she would take into account our pristine payment history and the fact that we'd only used the insurance for well visits in the five years we'd had it. Maybe the fact that we were in perfect condition and our recent physicals had put us in the healthiest one percent of all Americans would play some small part in her decision. She cleared her throat. She was going to help me. I could feel it.

"Sir, your policy is clear, and it's completely out of my hands. Have a good day, sir."

"But—"

"Have a good day, sir!" she said sternly.

"Have a good day? Are you seriously telling me to have a good day? This is going to cost me thousands of dollars I don't have. I'll guarantee you I won't be having a good day!"

"There's nothing I can do, sir. Good-bye."

And just like that, with the click of her phone, our lives were sent into a tailspin. The next few months would bring an avalanche of debt we wouldn't dig out from for years. The exponential fallout would change every decision and color every move we would make from that point on. For the next two years, Isabella would be cared for at the Mercy Children's Clinic, a Christian charity set up for disadvantaged and low-income children. They were kind and attentive, and they listened to our concerns about vaccinations. They never forced our hand on any decision but helped care for our daughter. I always felt they were doing God's work.

Our house sold. We successfully closed on the fixer-upper. We would have to live somewhere else for three months while we renovated the old, seventies ranch home. My beautiful, state-of-the-art studio was packed into boxes and placed in storage. The Mercedes had been traded for some sort of Honda, child-friendly product. This tiny Chinese baby had turned our perfect world upside down, but in a weird sort of way, I was excited about all this. I like new beginnings and second chances. Despite my dark side and my mean, defiant streak, which often gets me into trouble, I am, at the core, an optimist. I believe in the possible, in striving for things, and, yes, in dreams. I held out hope that this new house and arrangement would bring us a more efficient and manageable routine. Maybe Isabella would learn to walk here. Maybe she would sleep here. I believed it was all possible. So with no gigs on the books, no records to produce, and no songs to write, I threw myself into the renovation process of the home. I went to work every morning as if it were my job. We were temporarily living in my recently deceased aunt's empty house while I renovated the relic. I was up at 6:00 a.m., into my work pants, sweat shirt, and ball cap, and out the door by seven to the work site. By this time, we had no income at all and were living off old song royalties and the equity check we'd received from the sale of our Franklin home. It was all dwindling quickly. I was feverishly relocating walls and ripping up carpet and creating openings that didn't exist before. All of it was done to make the house more workable for Isabella and her unique requirements. When you're down on your luck, tearing things up is good therapy. I was making the sledgehammer sing. One evening, in the midst of the destruction, I got a frantic phone call from Yolanda.

"Regie, we're on our way to the hospital. I'm in the back of the ambulance. Isabella went into seizures again. Meet me there!" I dropped everything and immediately buzzed down to the Vanderbilt emergency room. They were wheeling her in. Another fever spike. Another grand mal seizure. This was gut wrenching. More forms signed, more doctors and nurses hooking her to more devices.

"Mr. and Mrs. Hamm, we're going to give Isabella a spinal tap right now," said the very masculine female attending physician.

"Is this something we absolutely need to do right now?" I asked. Once again, I had done too much reading. I had read that botched spinal taps could cause lifelong headaches. I was starting to wonder if my daughter would ever talk. She also showed a high tolerance for pain. Those two components, coupled with the fact that she was kinetic in her movements and a herky-jerky squirmy worm, made me nervous about someone trying to tap her spine in just the right way. I immediately ran through the worst case scenario of something happening we might never know about because she couldn't tell us. I saw her having lifetime migraines with no one on earth ever suspecting a thing for her entire life. So I pressed the doctor.

"You're worried about meningitis? Will the blood work rule that out? How long until it's back?

"Yes, sir. We're trying to rule out meningitis. The blood work could take ten minutes. It could take thirty."

"Why don't we give it ten more minutes before we jump into this?" I asked.

"Sir, you're not the doctor here. I am. I decide what we do and when we do it."

"Actually, doctor, since I'm her father, I decide. I'm not signing any wavers for ten minutes. If the blood work isn't back by then, you can do your tap." My blood was starting to boil. No one in this world-class medical facility had been able to give us any decent answers, and my anger and defiance was bubbling. Just then, she put her finger in my chest and pushed me out the door into the hallway. As I was being forced backward, I glanced at the clock on the wall.

"Now, you listen to me. If this kid has meningitis and I don't catch it immediately, this hospital is liable for a lawsuit that could put it completely out of business. That's not happening on my watch!" The doctor was half yelling at me now. "You can sign this waiver, or I'll call security and have you removed, followed by a phone call to child services—who I have on speed dial—and I'll have her removed from your custody for neglect and interfering with a medical procedure in a way that could threaten her life. I'm not even kidding! Your choice, sir."

"My wife can sign it. I'm not signing a damn thing!"

Yolanda signed the waiver, and the crew was rushed in. I stood in the hallway and listened to my daughter scream. As the team was performing its gruesome task, a young, perky nurse approached us in the hallway. "I have some blood work for Isabella," she said, sounding like a Southern cheerleader.

"That's her blood work?" I asked, looking back in at the clock.

"Yep. Are they doing a procedure in there?" she asked in a concerned whisper.

"Yeah, spinal tap. Hey, by the way, can you look at that chart and tell me if she has meningitis?"

"Yes, sir. It looks like … nope. No meningitis!"

I stared at the clock. Nine minutes—they could've waited nine minutes.

More forms. More signatures. We had been engulfed in the drama of the moment. But when the smoke cleared and once again no one could tell us what was wrong with this little girl, it began to dawn on me that this little slice of heaven hadn't been covered under any insurance plan. Not only was I on the hook for the last round, I'd be on the hook for this round as well. The stark reality sent a shock through me like a thousand tiny knives. My precious daughter, first child and absolute love, possessed some mysterious ailment. Not only could no one get to the bottom of it, I wouldn't be able to afford much more care. I started feeling like that wounded prisoner in the Robert Redford film *Brubaker* who waves the doctor off and says, "I can't afford no more."

It was close to Christmas now, and my sixteen-month-old little rag doll was still not sleeping through the night. With aggressive therapy, incredibly strict nutrition, and more hugs and kisses than can be measured, she was making painfully slow progress. She had learned to hold her head erect and sit up without assistance. She still couldn't crawl, grab a Cheerio, or utter any sort of coherent sound, but she could flash a smile that would melt your heart. Her ability to look a total stranger in the eye and smile with fearless abandon was a revelation to me. I watched her bring the bitterest of faces into full bloom on many occasions at the mall or grocery store. Despite her physical and mental challenges, she was a light everywhere she went, especially in our house. As much fatigue as my body constantly felt and despite the fog that permanently clouded my brain, whenever I walked in the door and heard her giggle, I was healed for a moment. The sheer work involved in getting her through a day was completely drowned by the her loving spirit and beautiful soul. As hard as it was, Yolanda and I never saw her as a drudgery or chore. She was a joy, and we were only focused on unlocking her from whatever prison her mind was in and setting her free from her physical chains. The frustration of that is tormenting. Watching your child flounder while other children are blossoming and saying the cutest things and jumping up and down on beds and getting in trouble for running too fast through the house and doing everything you always pictured in your parental visions is the most agonizing torture. This little girl who put so much happiness and love into the universe deserved to be whole. She didn't deserve the stares in public and the trips to the hospital and the torturous nights without sleep. I was starting to direct my anger toward God.

I phoned the doctor who, two years earlier, had miraculously helped transform my and Yolanda's bodies. We needed answers, and no one from China to Tennessee had been able to provide them. The conversation turned and turned. Immunizations were discussed. He speculated that her fresh immunizations in China may have been the culprit. China gets the leftover immunizations from the U.S. Theirs still have high amounts of the mercury additive (Thymerosol). We talked about the possibilities of complications at her birth. She was born in a very rural province and was most likely delivered in a house or a barn or God knows where. Maybe the umbilical cord had wrapped around her neck long enough to cause brain damage. The trouble was none of her brain scans had shown any signs of brain damage. The conversation turned to toxins, specifically mold. We knew the house we were currently living in had had a mold issue in the past. My mother had been diagnosed with mold issues. I knew a little about this; it would soon be an obsession.

"When did the seizures start?" he asked.

"We now think she was always having them, but the really big ones didn't start until we moved into this house."

"This is the house that has had mold problems?"

"Yes, sir," I replied, suddenly putting it together. I felt sick. This suddenly made all the sense in the world. I was making my daughter sick by keeping her close to mold!

"My bet is that she's reacting adversely to mold. You're going to have to keep her far away from it. Whatever you have to do, just get her in a mold-free environment."

Given my penchant for extreme focus (or, as my wife calls it, "being crazy") and locking in on certain things, I went straight to the Internet and began surfing. This was the first of what would eventually turn into literally hundreds of hours online researching mold. Mold was my new buzz word. I made arrangements the next day to move out of the house and into an apartment for the remainder of the relic renovation. I was on the phone the next morning with every mold specialist I could find in the phonebook to come out and inspect the relic. We had the flat house. Now it had to be a mold-free house.

The carpet was torn out, and there was sawdust and

construction material everywhere. This was the perfect time to figure this out. I started at the west end of the long, straight structure in my master bedroom, wall by wall. Black patches on any piece of Sheetrock meant the wall must be opened. I started seeing it where it didn't exist. I began tearing out board after board, wall after wall. There was only one way to see behind it: tear it out. I couldn't bring my delicate daughter into a place with a silent killer behind the walls. Room by room, wall by wall, I demolished yard after yard of perfectly intact Sheetrock and would then inspect every inch of the raw studs. My chronic lack of sleep was causing me to be more obsessed than usual. I tortured myself with thoughts of how mold could grow and how I could thwart it. I would stare for minutes at a time at walls and ventilation shafts. While construction workers buzzed around me, I would be standing in the middle of a room writing silent battle strategies for the dreaded fungus and its toxic growth, talking to myself under my breath, and darting my eyes from place to place. I had no less than three specialists inspect every inch of the house at various stages of its remodeling. Despite their reassurances, it was never enough. If the house scored seven out of ten, I needed it to be ten out of ten. If it was rated at about a C-plus, I needed it to be an A-plus. I could feel myself listing into insanity. All I thought about was mold and its toxic effects. I would walk through rooms smelling walls. Focus had turned to obsession. Concern had turned to extreme paranoia. We put in a four-thousand-dollar air purification system, which we couldn't afford. We did treatments to the underside of our floor joists in the crawl space. Everything we could think to do, we did. The bills were mounting, however, and the end of the money was in sight. Still no gigs, still no records to produce, still no songs being recorded, still no one interested in Regie Hamm. I wasn't thinking about it. I had a house to customize.

"Reg, here we go again. We're in the back of the ambulance headed to Vanderbilt. Meet us there," was the cell phone call I got that evening while tearing out a wall. Yolanda's voice was a little less dramatic than it had been the first time this call was made, but it was more solemn and serious. I snapped into action and dropped my tools, running through construction debris, leaving every light on. I was on edge now and feeling unstable. How many more times could we do this? How much could Isabella take? How much could *we* take? God was not talking to me anymore. At least, I wasn't hearing him. No more signs of irony or clever metaphors. I felt like I'd been used, like someone had walked up and said, "Here's some talent; you can't use it. Here's a dream; you can't chase it. Here's some money; you can't keep it. Here's an innocent little girl; you can't help her." That last part made my blood boil. I'd been processing my plight for the last few months. I had the official release form from Universal Records in a box down in the makeshift office. God wanted my dreams dead for some reason. That was fine. But now he was messing with my daughter, and that made me angry. She didn't do anything to deserve this. I was a self-centered, defiant, unruly smart aleck. I knew I probably deserved the spanking I was getting. She was a sweet, innocent angel who'd known nothing but sickness, turmoil, and confusion since the day of her birth. This was unacceptable to me. I'd always had an uneasy relationship with God in the first place. It wasn't uncommon for me to question his very existence on occasion. Now, he was straining the fibers of my tenuous belief again. I wanted to fight.

The late autumn sun was sinking as I bolted onto the interstate toward Vanderbilt Hospital and pushed the pedal to the floor. I was indignant and angry, staring aggressively like an agitated tiger and clinching my teeth. Finally, I erupted, "Seriously? This is all you've got? A baby? You have to do this to a baby?

What kind of sick, twisted narcissistic deity does this? You want me? Take me! I have nothing left, and I'm sure you're just fine with that! It's what you wanted from the beginning. We all have to bow down to the big, bad creator, don't we?" I was yelling now. "Do whatever you want to me. I don't care anymore!" Tears were streaming. "I'm a full-grown man. I can take it, but this is an innocent little baby, and she's been dealt nothing but horror and confusion and sickness since she was born! Why do you have to do that to her? I understand destroying me. I'm sure I've had it coming. But why her? It's not enough to destroy everything I've ever wanted; you have to destroy my daughter too? Too much! It's too much! You always have to break people like me, don't you? I can't be who I am and still be on your side! You force people like me to become pagans because we see through your bullshit! You demand everything, and then when we don't cooperate, you take it anyway! You know what? Job was a chump! You made a bet with his life! Who or what does that? Okay, so you got me. You did it. You stopped me from doing the thing I wanted the most. Fine! Who cares? It's a stupid career. It's just songs and music and frivolous crap that doesn't matter. But you made a mistake. You gave me something I love more than anything I've ever loved in my life, and I will not sit by and watch you do this to her. You owe me an explanation for this! I'm calling you on this one! You want my money? Take it! You want my career? Take it! You want my health? Take it! But stop doing this to my little girl. This is between me and you. She has nothing to do with it. She's being punished because of me and my self-ishness; that's not fair! Do whatever you want to me. Leave her alone!" I'm sure other commuters were confounded by the man covered in Sheetrock dust shaking his fist, pointing accusingly at no one, and screaming at the top of his lungs, but God and I had to get some things straight. You can't have a relationship with something or someone without honesty. Despite my many flaws, I've always known this as an artist, as a husband, and certainly as a father. Now, as someone wrestling with matters of the spirit and soul, it was time for honesty. In short, you can never have a real relationship with God until you scream and fight with him. I pulled into the all-too-familiar Vandy parking lot, wiped my eyes, and put my brave face on for my family. It was another night of wires and IVs. More tests. More drips. More medications. More questions without answers.

LEAVE SOMETHING BEAUTIFUL ALONE

*T*he months went by. Night after excruciating night of sleeplessness. There would be two, three, maybe four hours of silence and then the cry, and then we'd be up 'til daybreak. Days and weeks of trying to find answers and reasons for a career in shambles, a daughter in turmoil, and a life that had spun into something unrecognizable. We did finally move into the relic, unfinished though it was. We simply had to get on with life and had officially run out of money. The drip-by-drip renovation would continue on for years. I set up a meeting with my managers, who I hadn't seen in months. I hadn't been taking my vitamins; I couldn't afford them anymore. I'd replaced high-octane workouts with trips to Home Depot for plumbing supplies, two-by-fours, sheetrock mud, and everything that can be imagined. I hadn't touched a piano in weeks. I hadn't talked to anyone in the music business in I couldn't remember how long. I didn't know what I was going to be doing with my life anymore. All of my rock star accouterments had been stowed in my closet in exchange for work boots and paint-covered sweatshirts. I hadn't slept more than four or five hours at a stretch in almost a year. I felt like a wreck and had no idea what I looked like to the rest of the world.

I walked into the restaurant out of the wintery, Nashville air in a pea coat and toboggan. Unshaven and bloodshot, I'm sure I was nothing to behold. Stuart and Norbert were glad to see me and more than warm in their sympathy for what was happening in my life but were visibly taken aback by my appearance. The conversation was short and awkward. Finally, Stuart said, "Buddy, if you want to take another run at this, I'll be there with you all the way. When you're ready to lose the weight and go for it, I'm here." *Lose the weight?* I thought. I guess I didn't really know what had been happening to my body. I'd been staying alive and barely hanging on for so long, I guess I didn't realize I was slipping into atrophy. I'd lost my self-awareness and was singularly focused on my daughter and her well-being. There was no time for vanity and sometimes barely enough time for a shower. The stardom that had been so close to my grasp was now a million miles away. It felt like I'd fallen backward down a mountain and would never be able to get back up it. I was exhausted. Losing the weight and going for it were distant notions from another life. That was the last meeting I ever had with my management team. Several months later, they went out of business. That chapter was over.

The medical bills were staggering. The royalty checks we were living on were dwindling. There had been a time when the royalties just on all the songs I had already penned over the years would've sustained us for a year or two. People were now downloading songs, and the music business was crumbling. The infrastructure was contracting to accommodate tighter budgets. No one was investing. How in the world would they ever make their money back? Those little plastic circles we used to all get paid from were becoming obsolete as the primary delivery system of music. The CD was dead, and the thing replacing it wasn't being monetized. The business I had risen through the ranks of a few short years earlier no longer existed. Now, as a result of that, along with the natural sales waning over time, those royalties I used to take for granted wouldn't get us through the week. We'd cashed in every stock and retirement account we owned just to fend off the medical bills, but we still owed thousands. Isabella was unable to get on any government health care plan, state or federal, because we apparently made too much money. At one time, we might have, but now we were very close to being destitute. The irony was if I had completely shut down and stopped working or Yolanda and I had gotten divorced, Isabella would've qualified for government assistance immediately. Doing the right thing isn't always rewarded. The platinum card that had carried us all over the world and been so nonchalantly thrown on tables at expensive restaurants was now paying for baby formula and diapers and was about to be cancelled. I was selling studio gear to pay electric bills. The undoing was swift, steady, and sure. My ship was going down, and it was carrying my family. I felt like a failure as an artist, but most of all, I felt like a failure as a man.

What did I have left that might be worth anything? Maybe I could still write songs. I knew that the *American Dreams* project had been a critical success in Nashville. Many people told me I had a knack for storytelling and would be a natural at writing country songs. I'm a Nashville native. The music of the South runs in my blood, and I have deep reverence for its sacred heroes: Johnny Cash, Merle Haggard, Roger Miller, Kris Kristofferson—all major influences on me and my music. Although I had been touted as a pop writer, I was too influenced by gospel and country to really be hip in that world. The storyteller in me wouldn't allow me to write mindless love songs. The artist in me wouldn't allow me to go back to writing mindless Jesus songs. I was starting to feel like a man whose art didn't fit anywhere. But given my newfound disdain for Los Angeles and its disposable pop culture and my love for Tennessee and the warm embrace of home, I felt that I could shape what I did into something possibly accepted in the country music community. I had good friends who were doing well there. Many CCMers I knew had made the leap successfully into country music superstardom. I was no interloper and had too much respect for the music to be a pretender, but if there was anything about my music that might resonate with country fans, maybe this could be a home for me. So I put the word out that I was looking for a country publisher. There were no calls back.

I scrounged. I'd produce a custom record here, get an advance on a royalty check there. I finally started supplementing with the occasional live gig, but the bottom line was we were drowning, and as hard as I tried, there wasn't anything I could do about it. My work ethic wasn't paying off. I operate in a hit-and-heat business. I had neither. Every fear I'd ever had since beginning my professional journey was coming to fruition. People who used to hang out with me every week weren't returning my phone calls. Guys who'd told me to my face how great I was and how honored they were to work with me were ducking and acting like they didn't see me in clubs. I could feel the cloud over me. I just needed a break. I knew I could still work hard. I knew I could still ply my trade. I just needed to take care of my family.

Through some random events and fortuitous encounters, I got a chance. Mark Bright had come to Nashville to be in Christian music but just happened to end up as one of the biggest and most sought-after producers in country music, working with the likes of Blackhawk, Rascal Flatts, and eventually Carrie Underwood. He had been a fan of my CCM writing as well as the *American Dreams* record and was interested to see what I could do in the realm of country. I was honored. He offered me enough money to pay the mortgage, keep the lights on, and keep the baby fed. I jumped. Maybe this was a new chapter. Once again, the optimist in me had to believe. One year after losing my record deal, I signed a publishing contract to write country songs. The money was half of what I had been making in Christian music five years earlier, but it was steady, and for someone who had no track record in that genre, it was generous. I had never wanted to be a staff writer again. I still cringed at the thought of writing songs for other people, but I had hit the bottom. I was dangerously close to becoming the guy at the bar who'd had hits in the past but was now painting houses (not that there's anything wrong with painting houses—I'm just not good at it). This man was giving me a real second chance at songwriting for money. I was grateful beyond words and determined to make it work. Once again, I became a madman.

It's hard to express how difficult it is to be creative when you're chronically sleep deprived. After almost two years of night after night interruptions, my thoughts were constantly jumbled and hard to verbalize. That's death to a songwriter, where language skills are everything. On the other hand, you feel high all the time when you haven't slept, so for the first year of that writing deal, I was prolific. Ideas and songs were pouring out of a hazy brain. I found that five or six in the morning, while Isabella was playing in a playpen (after already having been up for two hours), was a pretty good time to write. The interference of coherent thought wasn't getting in the way and editing ideas. I'd spent thousands of hours learning how to do this. I could now just let it all flow. The years of learning and honing my craft were serving me well, I thought.

More doctor bills, no insurance, and income cut by more than

70 percent—unfortunately, in this country, that's a bad combination. I've never been a believer in socialized medicine or really socialized anything. I'm a hardcore American dreamer. I wrote about it. I made a record about it. I believe in the individual and in risk and reward and in capitalism and self-reliance and free markets and all those ideals I contend made America a beacon to the world. I had seen up close and personal the train wreck of communism. I was raising a little girl whose orphaned state was a direct result of a ruthless dictator's edicts. In the 1960s, Chairman Mao had decreed that every family in China should have as many children as they could physically produce. In his view, this would make China the strongest nation on earth. He assured them the state would always take care of them. In a few short years, they had plunged themselves into a humanitarian crisis of epic proportions and started regulating the number of children every couple could have. One ghastly dictatorial policy was followed by another. Each brought worse results and consequences. By the 1970s, China couldn't feed itself, hence my mother's constant, inexplicable warning to me whenever I was leaving food on my plate: "Children are starving in China." Although I could never wrap my brain around what that had to do with me and my leftover meatloaf, she was right. Children were indeed starving in China. My daughter had been one of them and was brought to America because of the social policy failures that led to that starvation. I wanted her to know the fresh air of freedom and be steeped in the traditions of liberty. I wanted her to be the beneficiary of self-determination. I always believed I was responsible for my own medical care and the funding of it. Having the collective, all-pitch-in-and-take-care-of-anything is a notion with which I've never been all that comfortable (outside of military operations and interstates). I believed this child's health care was my responsibility, and I had emptied all my

savings and investment accounts to pay those bills. But now the financial burden was becoming something I simply couldn't bear. With my new stipend, we put all the medical bills on monthly payments—a hundred dollars a month to this one, fifty dollars a month to that one, twenty dollars a month to another one, and so on. I figured it up once, and if I'd continued paying those bills at that pace, it would've been fifteen years before they would've been paid off. One more trip to the emergency room and that number would double. Another and it would triple. We needed an insurance plan.

Songwriters are private contractors and are not offered health benefits. The songwriter is the smallest of small business owners. For my entire adult life, I've been self-employed, and it's a daily battle with regulations and tax codes and everything under the sun. So much of American life and law is geared toward unions and those who work for large companies. The lone, self-starting dreamer is often out there on an island alone. In the world of health insurance, it's no different. No matter how many different ways we tried to spin it, no matter how many companies we talked to or how many health care professionals we met with, the end of the discussion was always the same: "We're sorry, Mr. and Mrs. Hamm. Because you're self-employed, a private policy will simply not cover Isabella, given her condition." What had that doctor written on her chart? To this very day, I still don't know, but whatever it was, it had turned our lives into a health care odyssey that wouldn't end for years. Because we still didn't qualify for any government assistance, the only option left for Yolanda and me was for one of us to go to work for a corporation. Yolanda stepped up once more into the breach. My beautiful, intelligent, Latin queen who'd been a professional with an expense account and surrounded by superstars found a job at a call center that would provide health benefits for a nominal number of hours worked. She applied, got the job, and started as soon as possible. This left me home throughout the day to take care of Isabella and fulfill my contractual obligation of writing songs. And so began the slog of shift work care giving.

We were up at three, four, or five (if we were lucky) with the baby. Yolanda would leave around seven. I would get Isabella fed and changed by eight or nine, sit her in a chair next to the piano, and go to work. Her precious, giggling face kept me inspired beyond my exhaustion. My song plugger was trying to set me up with co-writes, but the family schedule made it a difficult endeavor. Nashville is a town built on the co-write (songwriting collaboration), but I've always had a difficult relationship with it. For me, it's often been nothing more than an exercise in compromise. Sometimes it even caused me to end up writing things I would never have written about, things I had real problems with, like, I don't know, surrendering maybe. Now, it just wasn't physically feasible. My little rag doll, who had started crawling and could hold herself up in a playpen, wasn't a child I could just drop off at a babysitter. She had to be monitored all the time for seizure activity. She had to be fed and changed and clothed and cared for just like an infant even though she was almost two. She also had to be taken to therapy sessions and thrived on routine. She couldn't utter a word and had high pain tolerance. You might never know she was feeling bad or sick until she was seizing in the floor with a 105 temperature. She was a full-time job. Though we had the occasional well-meaning friend who came over to help and though my parents would come by once every other week or so, Isabella's care was completely on the shoulders of Yolanda and me. As she aged and grew, no one else could handle her. Her kinetic movements that constantly put her in danger made her a baby that must be watched at all times. One of us would have to be with her constantly. There was simply no other way. So I wrote by myself, hoping I could land a hit song with someone and justify this unorthodox approach to my publisher, the man who'd taken such a risk on me. Maybe it would give us a little breathing room. Maybe we'd get out of debt with the hospital or the IRS, another expense that had fallen through the cracks. Maybe, maybe, maybe. I'd gone from being powerfully in command of my career to simply hoping for something, anything.

Every day, I wrote. Every day, Isabella remained in her mental and physical prison. Every day, she sat in a chair in our front room and giggled at silly daddy making up melodies and lyrics. She didn't know I was desperately trying to be brilliant for her, trying to strike the right tone, the right chord, the right hook that would once again make the masses sing along and bring some relief to her tired parents. Every month the advance check would show up in the mailbox. I knew how the business worked. Without songs in the marketplace, earning money and paying back these advances, it would only be a matter of time before Mr. Bright's benevolence would cease. He would have no choice. I knew the clock was ticking. Every new day was getting me closer to the end of this second chance. I needed a hit. I needed a break. I needed sleep.

The kidney stones I had accumulated over the years finally decided to all come out at once. The details of the surgeries I went through in February of 2005 could be a book in themselves. Let's just say surgery to remove kidney stones is something you *never* want to experience in your life. I had three. The surgeries left me bedridden and high on painkilling narcotics for the better part of a month. Family and friends pitched in to help with Isabella. Yolanda took time off work. For the first time in almost two years, I slept. Once again, gory details aside, my movement was limited for weeks, so I watched TV, read eleven books, and thought. Laying in bed, I started actually processing what was going on with my little girl. The clouds that had shrouded my view were temporarily lifting, and some clarity was being seen. For the first time, I was realizing that she wasn't going to get better. She wasn't going to learn to drive. She wasn't going to bring homework home from school. I would never comfort her broken heart from some unrequited, high school crush, never drop her off at college, never walk her down a center aisle, never have a cigar with a son-in-law, never hold a grandchild. The weight of her future had not fallen on me yet. Now it was rushing over me like a tidal wave. All special needs parents go through a certain grieving process at some point. You have to let go of the child you thought you were going to have, the child you thought you could nurse back to normalcy, and accept the child you do have. Yolanda and I had been so focused on getting through days and weeks and months that we hadn't stopped to think about Isabella's life and what the realities of it would be; at least I hadn't. Somewhere in one of those dark nights, beneath the masked pain of recently extracted kidney stones, in the fog of narcotics, I began to cry. I grieved for this beautiful angel and the life she would lead. I grieved for all the times she would be made fun of behind her back. I grieved for the boys she would like who would throw her looks of disdain and contempt. I grieved for the conversations we would never share and the Christmas carols we would never sing together. I grieved for myself and the joy of music I would never be able to fully teach her. Just when the tears would stop, a few hours would pass, and they would come back more fierce and uncontrollable than the last time. Days went by. I cried. I'd be okay for a day or so, and then some cheesy commercial with a father and daughter would come on TV, and I'd start all over again. My friend Kent Hooper's daughter had just been born with some severe physical deformities. That made me more weepy. Once I was able to walk, I asked a friend to come watch

Bella so I could get outside and stroll the neighborhood. The afternoon air would calm me and level my emotions, I hoped. I hobbled down the driveway and onto the street. Rounding the first corner, I saw the special needs bus pass right in front of me—tears. I made another turn and suddenly the short bus was passing me again. I was sobbing. Another turn, short bus again. Still another turn, short bus. At this point, I stopped and put my hands on my knees. I was crying so hard I couldn't get my breath, tears and mucus dripping to the ground. Every time I looked up, that blasted short bus was driving by. Finally, it became comical. My tears morphed to hysterical laughter. "Ha, ha, ha, ha. I get it, God. I get it!" I yelled, walking and clapping. "Nice touch. Nice touch indeed. Okay. You're right. Time to accept this and get on with it." I walked back to my house and into the makeshift office and sat at my keyboard. I had been watching a special on the Leaning Tower of Pisa that week and how it would've been completely ordinary had it not started leaning. Its tragic flaw had turned it into a wonder of the world. Suddenly, a moment of clarity and a song...

If that tower wasn't leaning in Pisa,
It'd be just one more stack of fine, cut up stones.
If it wasn't going under, it wouldn't be a wonder.
I say leave something beautiful alone.
Now, Mona Lisa is almost smiling at something.
Why she never laughed out loud, Da Vinci only knows,
But after all these seasons, I guess a girl's got her reasons.
I say leave something beautiful alone.
Don't move a muscle.
Don't change a thing.
You're looking just about perfect in this light.
You're my favorite work of art.
And you don't need no doctoring.

When you think you look all wrong,

You still make me feel all right.

It's like that baby with his hands all in the icing.

He loves to get it everywhere,

He loves to put it on so before he knows he dirty, scared uptight and thirty

I say leave something beautiful alone.

Don't you move a muscle.

Don't you change a thing.

You're looking just about perfect in this light.

You're my favorite work of art, and you don't need no doctoring.

When you think you look all wrong,

You still make me feel all right.

So let all the cowboys keep on riding them fences.

Let all the prodigals keep coming back home.

Let the world keep turning.

My love for you keeps burning.

I say leave something beautiful alone.

Baby, I say leave something beautiful alone.

THE HOLY SMOKE
DOODAH BAND

*I*t had almost been a year since I'd signed the publishing contract. Despite the sleeplessness, kidney stones, stress, and construction, I turned in over fifty songs that year. Over half of them were written solo in a room with my baby girl looking on. I was working as hard as I could. Nothing was happening. Just before the first option period was up, I was called into the office at the publishing company. Mark walked in and sat down uncomfortably close to me. In my heart, I kind of knew what was about to happen. I'd heard about meetings like this, but I'd never been in one. These guys had taken a risk on me and told the town I was the next big thing. I had not delivered on that promise. It was the first year of no activity I'd ever had as a professional songwriter. Pip was about to be exposed for the fraud he was.

"Whatever you're doing or not doing, it stops right now." Mark lunged in. "You're supposed to be the golden boy with the magic pen around here. Meanwhile, everyone else at this company is kicking your ass. Figure it out. Do whatever you have to do to fix this, but it's time for you to stop messing around and get to work, my friend."

Work? Get to work? No one in my entire musical life, not even my father, had ever spoken words like that to me. I had always been the example of how to do it right. Publishers pointed to me as someone to aspire to when they had these talks with their failing writers. Surely he wasn't calling me out on my work ethic? He had no idea what I was going through. He had no idea how long it had been since I'd slept or since my wife and I had been to dinner together. He didn't know how many times I'd been to the doctor or the emergency room that year. My blood started to boil. My face was flushed and that cursed defiant streak reared its ugly head. I breathed in, breathed out, tried to collect my thoughts, stretched my neck from side to side, and struck. "I've been SESAC Songwriter of the Year four times. I've had twenty number one songs. I've been on thirteen million records. You don't like what I write? Drop me. You're not happy with my process? Drop me. But if you ever question my work ethic again"—I leaned in closer—"I'll hand you your damn teeth!" He was clearly taken aback. I was spinning out of control. I lunged up and left the office in a rage, heart palpitating, palms sweaty. What had I just done? This man was giving me possibly my last opportunity, and I was throwing it back in his face. This wasn't just about my wounded pride anymore; my little girl's future was at stake. The room was closing in. I was about to lose this publishing deal, and that would be the end of it. The trouble was, he'd struck the nerve—the one I had always protected, the one that made me continually feel inadequate, no matter how much success I had, the one that gave me flashbacks of playing gospel music in malls and on street corners and watching the cool kids walk by and laugh at me and my family, the one that made me keep my fists up all the time, the one that said, "You might be good enough for small-time gospel, but you're not good enough for the big time." I felt exposed. I drove home and prepared for the worst. I was certain there would be a termination letter in the mail in a few days. It never came. Mark, being the kind man that he was, somehow saw through my insecurity and desperation. He picked up the second year option in spite of my outburst—another year of mortgages paid, another year of food, another second chance.

I knew I had one year to prove myself, so I changed my strategy. I got back into clubbing and finding acts I could develop. If I could deliver an artist with whom I'd written most of the songs for a record, get him or her signed, and a record out, my catalog would start getting noticed, and maybe I could turn this thing around. As it was, the stench of my rotting career was permeating all of Music Row. When I'd first had hit songs years earlier, I was simply everywhere. I was playing all the time, writing all the time, in the studio all the time. This would be difficult with Isabella, but I was determined to will myself back into the flow of success. I turned nothing down. Almost every night, Yolanda would come home from work, I'd splash some water on my face and try to recover from having been up since 4:00 a.m., kiss my wife, and head out to a club or a session or a rehearsal or something. My health was bad. Since getting home from China, I'd developed a respiratory weakness and always seemed to be getting a cough. I consulted a good friend of mine who was a world-class singer about how to sing through a cough. "Only one remedy, Reg. Straight whiskey, no chaser. One shot will get you through one song, maybe two. It's the only thing that works." He was right. Now, I wasn't hanging out at clubs and in studios to try and be something anymore. I was working for my wife and child. When I drank, it wasn't in celebration. I was simply getting through a show. Period.

Coming up on three years without regular sleep was wreaking havoc on my body, Yolanda's too. She had always been so strong. I don't remember her being sick much before Isabella. Now, we were both susceptible to anything and everything. I suppose it's that way with most new parents. The problem here was even when Bella was sick, she couldn't sleep. That meant that when we were sick, we didn't sleep. Recovery of illness always felt temporary. The whiskey was getting me through shows, but I always eventually came home to a child that demanded my full attention. Months dragged on. The routine became a prison. There was occupational, speech, and physical therapy three days a week. Every night after dinner, we would walk her up and down the long hallway, believing one day something would snap and she would walk without assistance. Any night I wasn't working, I would take little Bella Boo to the mall and walk around with her while Yolanda rested up for the looming, sleep-disturbed night. I would hold her hands to steady her and slowly walk the length of the mall with her and then back again. On and on we'd stumble and trip and bump into people and fall and get two steps and freeze and lean and reset and try and tumble and then back again. We'd ride the escalator up and down, up and back down. I would watch her fledgling gait and try to figure out the answer. There were "cool" kids making fun of us in this mall too, I'm sure, but I didn't care about appearances anymore. Something was wrong with my daughter, something undiagnosed, something mysterious. I was doing everything I knew to do. Our nightly mall walks were actually just as good for me as they were for her. Countless times, she would look up at me and smile through her physical struggle. It always seemed to be saying, "Thank you, Dad. Thanks for helping and believing. I'm trying." That smile was the fuel I needed to continue on, no matter how tired or worried I might have been. In her smile, she seemed to know something I didn't. She seemed to be saying, "Everything is going to be all right, Dad." I wanted to believe it.

Days of waking up at four, dozing on the couch while she played in a playpen, cooking breakfast, writing while taking breaks to change diapers and hand feed lunches, working on the latest construction project, and then kissing Yolanda good-bye for the evening while I went to play some half-empty club were taking a strange toll. My daughter was a mystery. My life was a mystery. One night, after several long days of this, I came in late from a gig. By the time I got showered and into bed, it was pushing 2:00 a.m. I'd been up almost twenty hours. The whine started. Sometimes, if we let her just whine it out, she would fall back asleep; this wasn't one of those nights. Yolanda woke up out of her dead sleep and sighed. "Reg, can you get her for a while? I'll relieve you in a couple of hours."

"Yeah. I'm just getting to bed anyway." I was hazy and nauseated from no sleep. I knew Yolanda was too. There was no need in both of us being miserable. I staggered to her room quickly before she got into full scream. Opening the door, there she was, wide awake, holding on to her bed rails and jumping up and down. She was ready to play at 2:00 a.m. This was earlier than usual, and I knew it was going to be a long one. I picked her up and lay her on my chest.

"What are you doing up, monkey? You got to sleep sometime." I was trying to be sweet and attentive, but my voice was cracking from the gig, and my body was in severe fatigue. She was unusually restless and busy, making it hard to hold her still. We sat in the rocking chair in her room. "Come on. Let's talk about this for a minute. Settle down, monkey, settle down." She was squirming and fighting to get on the floor. If I put her down, she'd bang around all over the house and wake Yolanda. I was holding on tighter.

"What's wrong with you, baby? What's going on in that brain?" I said in a more concerned and urgent tone. My brows furrowed, and I felt like I wanted to cry. "Why can't you talk? Why can't you walk? Why can't you pick up a spoon? Why can't you understand me?" I said with my teeth clinched. I had put my hands on her head to massage her scalp. Somehow, in my convoluted, sleep-deprived mind, I thought putting pressure on her skull was the trick that would work. When your head is unclear and you've gone for a few years without uninterrupted sleep, you get strange thoughts and ideas. We had been brushing Isabella's skin every night for sensory issues. We'd been trying to get her to use sign language. We'd gone through more mold remediation than anyone I'd ever heard of. We'd stopped wearing cologne and perfume, thinking the chemicals were exacerbating her problems. We banished the dog to a different part of the house and didn't let him near her because of pet dander fears. Her nutrition was impeccable; she never had processed food, refined sugar, or flour. Everything she ate was organic and fresh. She got therapy three days a week, plus the work we were doing at home. We played classical music in her room every night. We read to her and nurtured her and went above and beyond in every way. The culmination of these things should've been producing a superhuman prodigy. What were we doing wrong? It was all too much to comprehend. I squeezed her head harder, thinking more pressure would be good.

"Why can't you talk to me? Why can't you sleep?" I pressed harder. "What is wrong with you? Your brain just needs some pressure; this will help." I was out of my mind and now crying edge-of-insanity tears. "Why won't you talk to me?" I was pressing her little head harder now and changing the question from

"Why can't you?" to "Why won't you?" She went from ignoring me to staring at me with concern.

"Why won't you sleep?" I said through hysterical tears and a tight jaw. I was pressing her skull too hard now, but I couldn't stop. "Just sleep for a while. Just say something!" I pressed harder. She furrowed her brow and showed a look of pain. I continued to press and tighten my grip. "You just need some pressure to relieve this little brain of yours," I kept saying. My brows were furrowed, and I was pressing harder and harder. "Why won't you talk to me, Isabella?" I kept asking through clenched teeth. Finally, her eyes started to well with tears, and she flashed the most terrified look I'd ever seen at me. I came to myself. Oh, God! What was I doing? I was killing her. My heart jumped, and a thousand knives shot through my skin. I released her skull and embraced her tightly. "Oh, God, baby, Daddy's sorry. Daddy's sorry!" She started crying in a frightened tone. This wasn't Daddy. Who was this man?

"I would *never* hurt you, Bella Boo, never! I just wanted to make your head better. I'm sorry, baby. Daddy's sorry!" We were both a wreck, and I was shaking from the thought of what I might have done with an ounce more pressure. I had to get it together. I was freaking out. Just then, Yolanda came in. "You want me to take over?" she said in a creaky voice.

"Yeah," I said, breathing deeply. "I think you'd better. I'm sorry, but I think you'd better."

This mystery was pushing me to the limit. I was playing in a southern rock band, doing solo club gigs, writing with artists, and trying to make anything happen, but nothing was working. The years of doing no wrong felt like some distant dream. I was invisible. I had become one of those no-name guys who bang around in clubs all their lives, trying to make it happen while time slips away from them. I was past my prime. I'd gone from number one parties and Vegas trips to a ceremonious ascension into pop stardom to playing forty-year high school reunion parties at the local bar, driving all night to do a show at a VFW for a hundred and fifty bucks, playing birthday parties and two-for-one nights. Every year, I believed we'd turn a corner and come out of the slump, but every year, it got worse. I still believed in the breakthrough and the dream and all of the things I'd put my trust in over the years, but it was all failing me. By the end of 2006, I'd stopped cutting my hair and wore bandannas everywhere. My wardrobe had been whittled down to two pairs of jeans and some sleeveless T-shirts. Every show was kicked off with a couple of shots of whiskey whether I had a cough or not. I was numb and rudderless.

Just before Christmas 2006, I drove with the southern rock band Smokey Lonesome to do a show somewhere in Illinois. I'd scrounged some seed money a year earlier to produce a CD for them, hoping we could get it signed to a label. The lead singer and I had co-written all the songs. If I could get them signed and get a single released to country radio, maybe my fortunes would turn. That dream, however, was quickly disintegrating. I had gone from writer/producer to side man/van driver. It was cold, wet, and grey, and I, once again, had a cough and no voice. I was sick and exhausted and about to play for two hundred drunken party-goers. As I drove the van filled with instruments north, I listened to the bass player and drummer tell war stories of the road. They were both seasoned pros, and their stories were good. I stared at the broken white lines, and my mind raced past thousands of my own stories from childhood to that very moment. We arrived at the metal building, unloaded, set up, and sound checked. Then came the long, excruciating wait until show time. As I've gotten older, I've grown to hate almost everything surrounding a live show except the show itself. For me, waiting for the lights to go down is the worst part.

After a few hours of pacing, a light dinner, and a change of clothes, show time was closing in. I walked, carrying my beloved bottle of Jack Daniels through the rowdy crowd, to find my place on stage. The lights went down, and the obligatory gasps and light screams cut through the air. I stared blankly at the locals, drinking, smoking, laughing, and waving their already half-drunken arms into the air to form the universal "rock 'n' roll" sign. I unscrewed the bottle next to me and took a long gulp. The deadening medicine burned as it went down and then warmed my face. I handed the bottle to the drummer who was sharing my riser. He took a swig and handed it back just in time for us to strike the first down beat in perfect time with the flashing stage lights. For the next seventy-five minutes, I would be okay and in my comfort zone. After every song, I took another swig of whiskey. I guess some find sloppiness in alcohol. I always found focus. I played and drank…and drank…and drank. I was numb, and that was just fine with me. Scanning the room through my sunglasses, I wondered how I'd gotten there. I was so far from singing songs about faith and mercy. I was a million miles away from my former rock star perch. I was a has-been songwriter banging out chords and rhythms to drink to. The night became a haze. Faces and bodies surrounded me on all sides, and the room was starting to look like one of those fun houses where strategically placed mirrors distort physical features and characteristics. The noise was dulling my ears, and I could hear a voice saying, "Look at you. You're a joke. You always were a joke, and now it's official. If you thought you were ever going to rise above your past, look around. Regie Hamm isn't even average anymore, much less anything above it."

The show ended. I signed things with the band, talked to

fans, and waited on my state of mind to normalize. Once I felt sober enough, I packed my gear and got back in the van to drive back to Nashville. I would be up all night, but I was used to that. One lost night's sleep among hundreds wouldn't make a difference now. As I drove through the drizzling rain with the drums and amps still ringing in my ears, I thought about the future and what, if anything, could be done to turn my fortunes around. I had ten months left in my career, and then my monthly stipend would run out. I'd done everything I could, but I knew finding someone to take another chance on me would be almost impossible. I was damaged goods as an artist and as a writer. Now the band I'd produced to try and will myself back into the game was going nowhere, and I was just a sideman. They call it being "snake bit." Once you're branded as that guy—the guy who can't deliver anymore, the guy who's old news—you're done. I could tell by how long it was taking people to call me back (if they called back at all) that I was snake bit. The show I'd just done was a fun night out for a lot of wonderful people in Illinois. The band I was playing with was stocked with amazing talent, and I loved those guys. The music we were playing was exciting and fun. Still, none of it was moving me forward. I was way past the age of playing all night in clubs with my buddies for beer money. I had real bills and a real family to feed, and I wouldn't be able to do that playing Legion Halls on weekends. If there was an answer out there, it was something I couldn't see at that moment.

DON'T KNOW MUCH ABOUT LOVE

*T*hrough a strange and random turn of events, in late 2006, we were offered the opportunity to adopt a baby boy. His teenaged birth mother had seen our Christmas card on a refrigerator and sought us out. She wanted a life for him she couldn't provide, and if we would take him, we could have him. This was the second time I had personally witnessed the greatest act of love I've ever seen. We'd always been opposed to domestic adoption, but we called within two hours and accepted him. Our time with Bella had softened us and shown us the importance of love, both giving it and receiving it. We knew before we ever saw his two-hour-old, bald head that this little boy was special and perfect and ours. No matter what condition he showed up in, we would take him and everything that came with him. As it turns out, what came with him was nothing short of amazing.

Raising a special needs child can grind your emotions into a state of hopelessness. All you see are other kids doing things yours isn't doing. The competition among parents is brutal when discussing where their little Johnny or Kimmie is in reading or math or walking or talking or sports or music or just about everything. There's a little stage mom in all of us when it comes to our kids, I guess. With a special needs child, you can only sit there and listen; you can't participate. "My little Topher is doing calculus and running for office already. Can you believe he's only four?" How do you respond to that? "Well, my Bella walked across the room today, didn't have any seizures, and recognized the color red!" That conversation doesn't play out well. Special needs parents really don't need anyone else holding a mirror up to their child's disability. They already know what the future holds. They know how advanced your little Topher is. They need a break, maybe a night out, maybe a weekend off. They need your little Topher to not turn his nose up when their child drools or falls in front of him. They need to know their child will be accepted in the world. They know that one day they won't be around to help. They know that one day this special child will be a part of the adult landscape and that scares them to death. While you're reciting all the new Topher accomplishments, they're not hearing you. They're just hoping Topher will be compassionate when he's older. They're hoping Topher will help make the world he creates a safe and inclusive place for their child. So it was with Yolanda and me. We were so engrossed in our struggle with Bella; we probably forgot to laugh sometimes. We might have forgotten to relax and breathe on occasion. My Gabriel Tice Hamm is the namesake of my wife's deceased father, Gabriel, and my PawPaw Tice, the man who switched foxholes on Iwo Jima. If Bella had given us new dreams, Gabe would give us new life. The grind we were in was about to get a breath of fresh air.

A chance and totally random encounter with my old friend Kevin piqued my interest. I'd known this man since neither of us were men at all. He'd gotten married in my parents' living room when I was just a teenager and was a holdover from that past I continually tried to put in the distance. He and his wife were in town and looked us up. Coffee was on the books. By this time, Yolanda had seen the demise of yet another company and was now working at Starbucks for insurance. It seemed like a natural place to meet. We met Kevin and his wife, old friends whom we hadn't seen in at least fifteen years, at Starbucks and began the obligatory ordering of latte this and frappe that. The small talk of another life was being retrofitted for this one. Packing entire lives into twenty minutes over coffee is awkward and incomplete. Bella was with us, and Kevin kept staring. "You know, Reg, she looks and acts just like Barry McDonald's son," he said, studying Bella's movements and demeanor. "His son has something called Angelman Syndrome. I'm telling you, she acts just like him." Barry McDonald was another old friend from another life. These people from my past were having an impact on my future, and I didn't realize it. We finished our drinks, gave hugs, and went our own ways. Angelman Syndrome wouldn't leave my mind.

I'd never heard of Angelman Syndrome before. It sounded like one of those things they just stick a name on when they can't figure out what it is—Epstein Bahr, Post-Traumatic Stress Syndrome, Fibromyalgia. When we'd left the coffeehouse and were back home, I bolted to the Internet and started surfing. Sure enough, there it was. I read the symptoms: "Individuals with AS have a movement and balance disorder which ranges from mild to severe. While some children with Angelman walk before age three, most walk much later and some never achieve independent walking. The movement disorder can be mild and only affect gait and hamper some fine motor skills, or severe enough to prevent self-help skills like feeding, walking, and dressing. Most individuals with AS have a seizure disorder which can be difficult to treat. Feeding disorders in infancy are common and some persist throughout childhood. Sleeping difficulties are commonly noted in individuals with AS. Individuals with AS tend to have a happy demeanor, characterized by frequent laughing, smiling and excitability. Many individuals with AS have an unusual attraction to water and take great pleasure in water based activities like swimming and bathing." This was my Bella. She fit the description to a tee. It was like I'd found the Holy Grail. Yolanda wasn't convinced, but we made an appointment with the Vanderbilt genetics department anyway. There was a six-month waiting list. We got on the list and prepared for a little boy to come into our lives.

Domestic adoptions can be sticky and uncertain. Gabriel's went off without a hitch. He was born quickly without extensive labor and responded to all the things he was supposed to exactly when he was supposed to. By all accounts, he was a perfectly healthy little boy. We breathed easy. The only drama he brought was a few weeks of colic, which brought with it no sleep. For a moment, we were panicked and concerned, but on the first night of his eighth week, he slept twelve hours. We woke up in a cold sweat and ran to his crib. We thought he was dead. We'd never seen a real, live child sleep twelve hours before. From then on, the kid was golden. The joy that child brought to us was healing and warm. Isabella was learning from him as well and picking up good habits. Something about the normalcy of Gabe and his development made all the drama we'd been living through for the last four years soften and melt a little. My babies were saving my life day by day. My career was freefalling, but it was okay. Answers were on the horizon.

The years were flying by, and 2006 was now 2007. Mark Bright had picked up the last year of my option in spite of the fact that I hadn't earned his company one thin dime. I've always been grateful to him for that. I know what he did, and I know he didn't have to do it. They say God takes care of fools and children.

I had been an annoying combination of both, and I knew God was keeping my family protected in spite of me. In the last year of my contract, I kept working and striving and playing and writing with nothing to show for it. As summer approached, I had only a few months of income left. For the first time in my life, I was making peace with the end of my music career. I knew I couldn't do more than I had. I had learned I couldn't make something happen. My thoughts weren't on songs or success anymore but on my family and the love that moved and breathed inside the walls of my unfinished house. True surrender was taking place in my heart.

The call came on July 3, 2007. Yolanda was out with the kids somewhere, and I was home alone. When I saw Vanderbilt on the caller ID, I knew what this was, and my heart started to race.

"Mr. Hamm?" asked the kind voice on the other end.

"Yes, this is Regie Hamm."

"Sir, this is Doctor Phillips with the genetics department at Vanderbilt." I knew exactly who it was and exactly why he was calling.

"Yes, sir, doctor. How are you today?"

"I'm fine, Mr. Hamm. We have Isabella's test results, and they are conclusive. She is showing a partial deletion of her fifteenth maternal chromosome."

"Angelman Syndrome?" I asked, not fully understanding the scientific jargon.

"Yes, sir, a partial deletion of the fifteenth chromosome. That's referred to as Angelman Syndrome."

"Thank you for calling me before the holiday, doctor. What's our next step?"

"Come in to the office after the fourth, and we'll give you some information and answer any questions you might have." I was silent; he was somber. "Mr. Hamm, I'm terribly sorry, sir. I wish it was better news. Please, if you need anything, don't hesitate to call our office," he said as if someone had died.

"Actually, Doc, I'm relieved. This news could be better, but at least we know what we're dealing with now. Thank you," I said politely, and that was that. I was elated. I took my first deep breath in five years. All the riddles answered. All the mysteries solved. We hadn't been bad parents; there was no mold problem; she hadn't been born prematurely and had the umbilical chord wrapped around her neck; she hadn't fallen off the bed while we weren't looking and gotten brain damage, and she hadn't had some reaction to too many immunizations. She was missing a piece of herself that was so small it couldn't be seen with the naked eye, but so fundamental it imprisoned her in a world all her own. In a strange way, I could kind of relate to that. Yolanda and the kids came busting in the door. I just stared.

"What?" she asked.

"I just got off the phone with Vanderbilt," I said, holding my gaze.

"She has it, doesn't she? She has Angelman Syndrome, doesn't she?"

"Yes, she does."

"Now what?" she said in a relieved tone.

"Now we celebrate the Fourth of July and on Monday start finding out everything we can about this. We also find everyone we can find in the country who has it. Now that we know what it is, we can attack it."

"Yes, now we know. It actually feels good to know." We had done our grieving. We wanted to paint a target on whatever Isabella had and shoot at it. Now we knew.

Summer passed. My last day of income would officially be September 1, 2007. Knowing what to call Isabella's condition didn't make the days easier. The grind was still the grind, and it always would be. Knowing we had an Angel—the nickname given to children with Angelman Syndrome—didn't change the fact that I still had to go out and earn a living somehow. I pressed on 'til the end. A month before my contract was up, I had several long conversations with my song plugger, Kelly King. In our last conversation, she told me something I'd never heard in my life. Not since I was five years old, playing drums for altar services in my dad's revival crusades, had anyone ever implied to me that I might not be doing the right thing with my life. I always thought my unquestionable destiny was one of music and art. I'd struggled through impossible terrain and wrestled my own demons to continue that path. What Kelly said to me shook me to my core.

"I don't know, Reg. Maybe you've had your time. Maybe you've gone as far as you can. Maybe it's time to rethink what you do. I don't have the answers, but it might be something to think about."

There was a time I would've gotten my back up and allowed my defiant, two-year-old self to come back at her with some venomous retort. This time, I had surrendered to the realities of my life, and I listened with an open mind and heart. Maybe she was right. Maybe this was an opportunity to do something different I'd never thought about doing. One thing was certain: after September, I had no idea how I was going to be feeding my family or paying my mortgage. Pip was running out of time as a gentleman. I thanked her for her time and patience with me, and we said good-bye.

I made arrangements with my banker to take out a home equity loan to finish the house once and for all and effectively live on. We wouldn't close until December, but that would get us through Christmas and into the new year. I had drummed up enough work for November. October was the wild card. I pressed. I'd been in touch with some jingle houses and was doing some work for a small one in Knoxville, but they were done for the season. I chased every lead I could chase, but there just wasn't work out there for me. There were no more royalty wells from which to draw, no more accounts to raid, no more credit cards to juggle, no more anything. We were debt free except for the house and the medical bills and the IRS bills. We drove old, paid-for cars. We didn't eat out or go to movies. But we still had kids that needed food and shoes. We still had electricity and phones. Even if I'd gotten a job, I wouldn't have gotten a first check in time to stave off the impending disaster. On October 1, 2007, my family would officially be broke—no food in the refrigerator, no electricity, no gas money to get anywhere, everything two months behind—broke. So I scoured the Internet every night for job openings. I now knew that it would be devastating to move Isabella out of the county, so I hung on and looked for jobs in my area. There was nothing but entry-level stuff that wouldn't totally cover our monthly bills. I was creeping up on middle age and unqualified to do anything other than what I'd been doing the past twenty years. Surrender wasn't a choice anymore.

The cool, autumn day was perfect when I walked to the mailbox. I used to love these walks. There were days I'd walked to the mailbox and opened envelopes with checks for more money than I now made in a year. These days, the correspondence was usually IRS notices and bills from Vanderbilt. On this October afternoon, there was a strange-looking envelope addressed to Yolanda and me. I didn't recognize the return address, but I casually opened it. Inside, I found a handwritten letter from the pastor of a church in California. I hadn't seen the man in thirty years. My family visited and worked at his church when I was a kid. My wife's family had been friends of his when they all lived on the coast. The note was matter-of-fact and to the point: "We heard about your daughter and wanted to help. Please accept this in love."

I was perplexed by the note until something else fell out of the envelope: a check for the exact amount we needed to pay all the monthly bills and keep the family fed until November, not a penny more, not a penny less. It was a miracle. I just fell to my knees in thankfulness and stared at the check and the note. The pride in me wanted to send it back and say, "No thanks." But I knew we wouldn't survive the month without it. I'd never been that guy, the one who needs assistance or puts his family in dire straits. I'd always been the benevolent gift giver. Yolanda and I used to anonymously buy people's meals in restaurants. We sponsored families at Christmas, donated cars to churches, and adopted Chinese orphans. I never knew what a charity check looked like. This was one of those miracles I'd heard about in my youth, the kind where God saves you just in the nick of time. Now my own family had been pulled from the cliff. Surrender was starting to make more and more sense to me. It was also becoming my only option.

The November work came through and paid. The home equity loan came through just in time for Christmas. On December 25, 2007, Isabella went into cluster seizures, meaning one every five minutes or so, and her fever spiked. We spent Christmas Day in the Vanderbilt emergency room again. More wires, more IVs, more tests. This time, though, we had a few more answers. By the time we got home with her, Christmas was over and so ended 2007. What would 2008 hold? How would I make a living? How many more ER visits would we have? After six years of this, I really didn't think things could get worse or more uncertain.

THE BLOG

By the beginning of 2008, an average day in our home was anything but average. I'd begun blogging on my Web site and trying to remain creative. I tried blogging about life with Isabella once. It was so long and exhausting I never posted it. To this day, I have trouble reading it:

The all too familiar whine starts between four thirty and five in the morning. It sounds like something between a cat's meow and a baby in distress. I've been hearing it now for over six years. The voice has gotten deeper and more mature over the years, but the inflection is still the same. It jolts my wife and I both out of a dead sleep. It doesn't happen as often as it used to. There was a time when this happened every night for months at a time. Now, it will only happen once every few days or so, sometimes not for a whole week. There are stretches when it doesn't happen for a whole month, but it still happens enough to throw our sleeping patterns off for weeks at a time.

My wife sighs in an angry tone. It feels directed at me. She knows I'm going back to bed and is resentful. She had been asleep for two hours when I came to bed, and I am resentful. Neither one of us has sympathy for the other any more; we're both just too damn tired. My heart is racing while I try to reconcile the dream I just came out of and the nightmare that is just beginning. I've been in bed exactly three hours. I can't focus. It feels like someone blew sand in my eyes. I throw the covers back and stumble in the darkness for my sweatpants and T-shirt, bumping in to walls and stubbing toes on my way to the next room. My wife sits on the edge of the bed and tries to collect herself. The whine happened fourteen minutes before her alarm was to go off. She is running her fingers through her hair and cursing under her breath. A pounding headache has been nagging her for three days, and it's throbbing worse now. She's so exhausted that I barely recognize her personality sometimes. She's on to the bathroom, in to her closet, and off to open a coffee shop. If she doesn't do this at least four mornings a week, my daughter's next trip to the emergency room will throw us back into crippling medical debt. Because of a tiny loophole in our private insurance plan, our eight-month-old, newly adopted daughter wasn't added to our coverage six years ago. Once it was discovered that she had a rare, preexisting condition, no private insurance plan in the country would touch her. I'm self-employed. My wife agreed to go to work for a corporation that only requires a twenty-hour-a-week commitment for full coverage. We're happy to have it, but our daughter is a full-time job, and the toll this grind is taking on the two of us is debilitating and aging us quickly. We have no help, and we both need sleep.

I'm racing into my daughter's bedroom to remove her customized bed constraint, calm her, change her, and bring her to bed with me before she wakes up my son, sleeping in the next room. If I'm not there within a few minutes, the whimper will become an inconsolable scream. We know all too well the domino effect of events that will take place if we don't quiet her in time. I raise the plastic, PVC bed constraint I spent ten days and over a thousand dollars to create and build and lift her from her tousled sheets. She is dead weight and offers no help whatsoever. She doesn't latch on to me. She doesn't wrap her arms around my neck. She flails and stretches and pulls handfuls of my hair violently while I carry her to her oversized, makeshift changing table. She's heavy and sleepy and trying to reach the floor for a stuffed animal over which she's obsessing. I lay her on the table and in one motion, grab the object, place it in her hands, caress her hair, and kiss her cheek to settle her. I look in her eyes and remember why I do all this. I'm trying to untie the double-knotted drawstring sweat pants she sleeps in. We found out years ago that if she sleeps in anything easily removed, we may walk in her room to find excrement painted all over her walls, sheets, and face. That's a two-hour cleanup, and sometimes a carpet cleaning machine is required. After untying the double knot and removing the sweats, I realize that her diaper is rancid and soaked. The damage a six-year-old can do to a diaper is repulsive and the very last thing you want to be greeted with at five in the morning. I am completely unfazed by the sight and smell. I've been doing this now for over six years. I could do it while eating a sandwich. I use all my powers of dexterity to hold her octopus hands over her head with one hand and maneuver the soiled diaper with the other. If I don't restrain her hands, she will reach down, grab a handful, and finger paint herself and me with the nocturnal production. Strength and clarity are required. I have neither, but I'm working the problem as fast as I can. Speed is the key. She is kinetic and flailing her arms and legs. I get the diaper off and a wet wipe on her bottom. Just then, my wife walks in and grabs the diaper. "Got it," she says in a cold, unflinching voice and disposes of it in a professional, nurselike manner. We are both emotionless and deadpan. This has been daily business for us for years. We've been working on her potty training for three years and are finally doing well. Early mornings are still the wildcard.

I put a new pull-up on her and new pants, all the while blocking her from grabbing the lamp next to me, pulling drawers out from beneath her, and sliding off the customized mat. After my daughter is cleaned and redressed, I carry her back to the bedroom with me to hopefully sleep a couple of more hours—hopefully. As I struggle down the dark hallway with her, she beats on the walls. I try to position her where she can't do it in order to keep my dog from barking and allowing my son to remain asleep. We get to the bedroom without incident. I place her in bed next to me.

My wife is off to work. I'm trying to will my daughter back to sleep with an attempted cuddle. Sometimes she falls back asleep. Most of the time, she doesn't. "Please don't let it be one of those mornings, God," I say under my breath. She is chewing on the pillowcase tag and kneeing me in the stomach over and over from her constant jerky movements. It's going to be one of those mornings. She grabs my arm and pushes it toward the remote. "I can't listen to it again," I say in my head. "I just can't do it!" She starts throwing pillows and shaking her head back and forth, screaming under her breath at me in unintelligible groans and slapping at me uncontrollably. I give in. I turn on the TV, scroll through the DVR, and play an episode of Barney. She screams with delight and settles down to watch the cursed, purple phenom dance around and spell things. I have twenty-seven minutes until my daughter freaks out again if I'm lucky. I'm not going to be lucky today. For the next hour and a half, I start a new children's program every thirty seconds. She's in one of those moods where nothing satisfies her, and if we don't start something new, she will go on a rampage through the house, waking up my son, emptying garbage cans, pulling things out of the refrigerator, beating on the TV screen in the living room, and a host of things I can't even anticipate. In order to keep stillness and some semblance of order in the house for the next hour or so, I work the remote at her every whim. I'm exhausted. I can't stand the voices and colors coming off the screen, but she is calmed by them. Finally, she settles into an animated movie. She's transfixed. I have a window of time. I leave her long enough to get her lunch, which must be cut a certain way for her to be able to eat it, and backpack ready for school and start breakfast—two eggs and a buckwheat pancake. I can make it in seven and a half minutes. The skillets are hot, and the materials are frying. Just then, I hear her running down the hallway. She is carrying the king-sized bedspread with her and chewing on it. She's running around the house, grabbing pictures off the walls, opening drawers, and raking the floor with her hands. This behavior usually signals oncoming illness. It's maddening. She's had pneumonia twice and strep three times this school year. When she's out of school, my wife or I have to be home with her at all times. She has to stay in our sights at all times as well. High fevers trigger seizures in her, and she can't be left alone for a minute. As much as I love her with every fiber of my being, she's completely and totally exhausting in every conceivable way, sick or well.

When breakfast is on the table, her medication is placed next to it and her backpack at the door. I chase her through the house, catch her, and lift her onto her customized, cushioned dresser top, and change her into her school pants while she tries to kick them off. She thinks it's a game; I don't. I carry her into the kitchen and place her in a high chair she should've outgrown four years ago. She must be restrained and controlled or I'll be cleaning maple syrup off the hardwood into the afternoon. I give her a stuffed toy to chew, and it settles her down long enough for me to begin feeding her breakfast. I give her anti-seizure medication with the first bite. I watch her swallow. It's down. I hand her a plastic water bottle to wash down the bite. I turn my back just long enough to hear the thud. She has thrown the bottle across the room and is laughing diabolically. While I'm down cleaning up the water, she grabs my hair and yanks, again with the sinister, evil nemesis laugh. I forget to move her high chair back to a safe distance from her plate sitting on the bar, and while I'm disposing of paper towels, she reaches the plate with the eggs and pancake and throws it on to the floor as well. She is now in the throes of hysterical laughter, and I'm back on my knees cleaning up eggs and maple syrup and salvaging what I can of breakfast. How did I get here? How long can I do this? My daughter is growing physically but not mentally. Will she be throwing eggs across the room when she's twenty-five? I can't remember what the beach looks like. I can't remember the last movie I saw. What am I doing today? What day is it? What if this house has radon? Remember to call the radon inspector. Oh my God, what if we've had radon for years and we're all carrying cancer? A house just down the street had radon. A young woman down the street was just diagnosed with lymphoma! That's not a coincidence! This whole neighborhood was probably built on a landfill! I've got to get a complete physical soon! My precious Gabe! He had some bruising on his legs last night when we gave him a bath. Leukemia! It's all falling apart! What if we get attacked with a suitcase nuke? How would I be able to care for Isabella in a world destroyed by a nuclear blast? What if there is no running water? What if we couldn't get her medication and she went into a seizure and never came out? What is radon? What time is it? Why am I on the floor? Just then, the phone rings, and I snap out of the wormhole your mind slips into when you're sleep deprived. Disjointed and troubled thoughts fly through your brain at the speed of light, and you freeze for thirty seconds or so. I need sleep.

I raise up to dispose of the refuse for the second time, only to catch a glimpse of myself in the window. That can't be me. I'm thinner than that. I don't know who that is looking back at me. Prolonged sleep deprivation throws cortisol levels off. You crave carbohydrates and can't seem to level your weight no matter how much you work out or eat right. I haven't had refined sugar in seven years. I live on salads and water. I've worked out five hard days this week. I'm fatigued, not energized. I'm exhausted, not refreshed. I feel like I'm dying. I throw the soiled eggs in the trash and answer the phone. It's my manager. I can't afford a manager. My manager can't afford to work for me, but he does anyway. I can't afford not to have a manager. If I didn't have a manager, I would be completely out of touch with my professional life. I so desperately want to make him a wealthy man. Right now, I can't even focus on what he's saying. Something about my Web site. Someone asked about a song of mine somewhere. There's a date booked December somewhere. He just said it, and I can't remember what he just said. My daughter has reached onto the bar, found my wife's fashion magazine, and has ripped ten pages out it. There's John Mayer on the floor. I wonder if he was up at five cleaning dirty diapers. I wonder if he even knows how to operate his oven. I can't help but imagine all of the amazing things he's been doing for the past six years. Our debut records came out the same year. He's an international superstar. I'm cleaning fashion pictures of him next to the starlet of the month up off the floor and spoon-feeding a six-year-old with special needs. I feel sorry for myself and ashamed of myself at the same time. I'm exhausted. Another wormhole. I snap back and tell my manager, "I'll have to call you back, Ed." He says okay, and I continue on with breakfast.

At ten minutes 'til eight, I change my daughter's shirt, brush her hair, put her shoes on, and brush her teeth while she pulls my hair. She gags on the toothpaste, and I stand perfectly still, staring at her. Is she going into a seizure? Is she going to throw up? Is this just the gag reflex most angels have? After staring at her for fifteen seconds, I determine she's okay, take her out of the high chair, walk her to the front door, blocking her hands from pulling down decorative candles and small pieces of furniture, and we descend the driveway toward the waiting special needs bus. Miss Dorothy and I help her on to the bus, they restrain her in her special seat, and she's off to learn how to sort colors, walk down a hallway without assistance, and show someone a picture of a water glass when she's thirsty. If she doesn't have a seizure at school and I don't have to go pick her up, I'll have exactly six hours to get in a workout, have lunch, and get any business that must be done during business hours done.

I get my son up, washed up, changed, and eating his breakfast of banana and rice milk. While he's feeding himself and watching a Disney production of some kind, I'll take ten minutes to step into my office and figure out the day. Most of the time, there's too much to get to. Things that used to take a week now take months. Time is moving in molasses. E-mails are first. "Okay, so, you haven't responded. I guess you don't have time for us little people anymore, but..." Delete. I don't read any further. Walk a mile in my shoes, and you'll know why it takes eight weeks to return a call or an e-mail. I don't feel human. I need sleep. In the last few years, I've had to make choices about how my time is spent. It certainly won't be spent dealing with someone else's passive aggressive inferiority. No time. Next. Two e-mails from my manager detailing what he was trying to tell me on the phone. Short and to the point. God bless him. He understands my life.

I respond with as much clarity as I can muster and move on to the next thing.

My wife, who's been working since 5:00 a.m., is listening to a customer complain about her latte. She's freshly coifed and pampered, and the biggest problem she'll face today is the wrong kind of milk in her overpriced coffee. My wife is working around kids half her age and with half her education, and she is trying to focus on getting the coffee right. Every cup pays for the insurance we cannot live without. Every upgrade insures that the next ambulance will be at least 80 percent covered. Every satisfied customer means the numerous trips to the doctor will be taken without thinking twice about how much money we have in the bank. She smiles at the young, well-kept, blonde woman rolling her eyes and replaces the precious latte. In another life my wife would be the one complaining about the latte. In this life she's choking back everything she wants to say to the ungrateful woman and simply says, "Have a nice day." The whole time she's thinking of our daughter and how she must keep this job. Nothing more.

At ten she's off work, and she and I meet at the gym. The gym is our one refuge; it keeps us relatively sane. There's a daycare center there where my son gets to play with typical kids, observe normal childhood behavior, and be around children who jabber back at him when he says hi instead of staring at him blankly. Today is a cardio day for me; I begin running on the treadmill. Five years ago, I could run three miles in twenty-four minutes and barely break a sweat. These days, I'm lucky to finish three miles in thirty minutes. I can push through it; I can get there. My daughter needs me to be strong and alert. My kids need me to live. I can't die. I have to do this. There's a hot shower waiting at the end of this; I can do it. The TV screens are filled with morning news shows and sports highlights. As the blood races through my brain, I start to get clarity on what the day holds and what must be done. I begin to focus and think like a normal human for the first time in five hours. My workday hasn't even started. At the end of the three-mile run, I stumble off the treadmill, past the mommies trying to lose that ever-present fifteen pounds, and into the shower area to collapse into the steam room. As the eucalyptus-laced steam rises into my nostrils, I close my eyes and pretend I'm in the spa at the Mirage in Vegas. Those were good days. After this I'll get dressed, have lunch at that new place in the MGM, and then shop and gamble the day away. Tonight, dinner and a show and as much sleep as I desire. The steam stops, and I'm back in reality. Hurry up and shave; clock's ticking.

My wife, son, and I go back to the house for lunch. We always have lunch together unless I have a business lunch. It's our time to have some normalcy with our son without the sporadic chaos that surrounds mealtimes with our daughter. There's no throwing of food or obsessing over plastic or constantly pouring water on everything. It's quiet and peaceful and nice. It's also the first time my wife and I have talked today. We catch up on household business, eat a couple of sandwiches, and press on with the day. She'll try and nap for an hour or so; I'll try to get three hours of work done before my daughter gets home. Once she comes home, it'll take both of us to handle both kids. I need to be working quickly and packing as much as I can in this three-hour window. Instead I find myself drifting and slow. I have a hard time focusing and being creative, knowing I only have a couple of hours before I hear my wife jerk the office door open and half-yell down, "Can you come help me, please?" I need to be able to work. I need sleep.

While having lunch, the phone rings, and my wife looks at the number. Her face drops, and I know who it is. It's the school. "Oh my goodness! Do you have a fresh shirt? Is she comfortable? Okay, okay. We'll be right there."

"You've got him. Bella started throwing up at eleven and had two seizures in the school nurse's office. I'm on my way. I'll call the doctor on the way to her office. See you this afternoon." We're now in crisis mode. My son will take a short nap, and I'll try to work, but I won't get anything done. I never do on days like these. They happen far, far too often. It's only twelve thirty. I need sleep. I change my son and get him down for his nap. He's such a godsend. He's normal and healthy and predictable. I know that when I go back in his room in two hours, he won't be having a seizure or a fever spike of 105. In a way, he's our little two-year-old rock. We depend on him. We count on him to be there. He's the one place we can always land and feel somewhat sane. He's a normal two-year-old. As challenging as that's supposed to be, it's a welcome change for us. It's not uncontrollable obsession. It's not knocking over end caps in the grocery store and then pulling the glasses off the checker in line. It's not chewing on a towel all day until it's so saliva soaked it has to be thrown away. It's not repetitive circles through the house, unplugging the living room lamp, taking trash out of the trash can and throwing it on the floor, opening the refrigerator door, throwing all the pillows off the couch in the den, lifting the rug in the living room and chewing on the rubber rug stabilizer, taking mail off the bar and ripping it into pieces, grabbing forks out of the drawer. Once it's all cleaned up, doing it again. Once it's all cleaned up, doing it again for three hours. For us, the terrible twos have been pleasant and peaceful.

While trying to be a genius behind my keyboard, I'm fielding phone calls from subcontractors who are calling for details of the next phase of construction. I'm building a 1,000-square-foot apartment for my mother-in-law above my garage. Today, it looks like we have a plumbing problem. The painters aren't here. I forget to call them back because I suddenly find myself talking about copper pipe, hot and cold lines, and making three trips to Home Depot in an hour and a half. All the while, my cell phone is going crazy with calls I can't take because I'm trying to understand what in heaven's name the plumber is talking about. It makes little sense to me, but apparently it's going to cost fifteen hundred dollars. At three fifteen in the afternoon, I haven't gotten any work done, and my daughter will now be home for the next two days. My week is essentially over.

At three forty-five, my wife and daughter get back from the doctor's office and walk up the sidewalk to the front door. Once my daughter is inside, the chaos will not end until 8:00 p.m. My wife calls this time of day crunch time. The first thing done is my daughter's bath. Bath time with her is stressful. She won't lift her hand or leg or foot on demand. It's a water-in-the-face, wet-from-head-to-toe, fight-for-every-piece-of-clean-flesh wrestling match. She stays on her hands and knees, face to the water. She constantly thrashes at it with her hands and laughs uncontrollably. She's obsessed with water. As she gets older, giving her a bath becomes harder and harder. I'm not sure what we'll do when she's fifteen or twenty or forty.

I go to Walgreens and pick up the prescription while the kids eat dinner. After dinner, they'll want to play. I've been up since four. I'm dead. By seven thirty, they have snacks and are off to bed by eight. We say prayers, kiss good night, and tuck in. Yolanda and I brief each other on the next day's events, and I walk downstairs to my office to work. It's 9:00 pm. I work and write and return e-mails and scour the Internet for jobs until 1:00 a.m. This all starts again in four hours.

ANGELS WAITING ON WINGS

For years, Isabella had been treated and studied by every specialist we could find. She'd been analyzed by rooms full of psychiatrists and psychologists, under the constant care of neurologists, and monitored weekly by more therapists than I can remember. She'd been diagnosed as severely mentally retarded. She'd been placed in the autism spectrum. Some said she probably had a form of cerebral palsy. We'd speculated on everything from mold reactions to brain damage. Now, we knew at last the name of her condition.

What we soon found was that no one in the mainstream medical world had much of an idea about what it was or how to treat it. The lack of medical knowledge about this disorder was depressing and eye-opening. If my daughter could be summarily thrown into the autism spectrum without the suggestion of a genetics test, how many other children had this disorder without their parents' or pediatricians' knowledge? How many children with autism were actually victims of wounded genetics? The first step was to connect with other families who had Angelman children. I was on the Internet and phone almost daily, tracking people down all over the country. I found other families through social networking Web sites and contacted them cold. I would leave my phone number and ask for theirs. Yolanda and I needed answers, and we needed to connect with others who had been through the same experiences.

I got the phone number from someone on the Internet of a woman with an Angelman son who actually did Angelman Syndrome research at Vanderbilt. Unbelievable! I had been at that facility hundreds of times, seeing dozens of doctors and specialists, and there was woman somewhere on that campus that could've cleared the mysteries up in moments. I had to talk to her.

Terry Jo Bichell answered her phone on the third ring.

"Hello. Is this Terry Jo?" I asked.

"This is Terry Jo," she answered in a sweet, thoughtful tone that was already comforting to me.

"My name is Regie Hamm, and I have a daughter with Angelman Syndrome. I've heard you have a son with it, and I'm just trying to meet everyone I can. Do you have time to talk?"

"Always! Tell me about your daughter," she responded.

We spent the next forty-five minutes discussing Angelman Syndrome, the details of the symptoms, the diagnosing of it, and the personal struggles with it. We talked about the research being done, and she told me about a man who had actually cured Angelman Syndrome in a mouse years earlier, right there at Vanderbilt. The cure was complicated and light years away from a human application, but it was the first time I'd heard anyone talk about hope and possibilities as it pertained to Isabella, and my adrenalin began to rush. She asked what Isabella could do and what she couldn't do. She was amazed to hear that Bella could walk and even run at such a young age, feed herself, and obey some commands. After years without sleep, through trial and error, we'd discovered ways to get her through the night most of the time. It all piqued Terry Jo's interest. "I have to meet this little girl," she said. "Let's get our families together so you can meet my son Louie." I gave Yolanda's cell number to her and explained that Yolanda was the social director and calendar keeper. I just carried things and paid for stuff. She and Yolanda set up a lunch at their house. We were about to meet the only other Angel we'd ever known.

Weeks later, we arrived at the Bichells' home and ascended the stairs of their historic, Civil War–era farmhouse with great anticipation. I knocked at the door, holding Isabella still while Yolanda bounced baby Gabe on her hip. A little boy no older than seven or eight opened the door with jerky, awkward movements. Upon seeing us, he squealed in delight and made those same unintelligible moaning sounds my Bella Boo made. We stared in amazement. As we entered the home, Isabella got away from me, ran up to him, and they touched each other's heads in an attempt at a hug. It was almost as if they'd known each other for their entire lives.

Louie walked like Isabella and had the same ability to bring chaos into a room. I sat in the living room and surveyed the surroundings. The strewn toys and chewed furniture made me smile. It was all too familiar. The conspicuous lack of frivolous decor also rang true. Nothing small or delicate can be displayed in an Angel home. Angels often swallow small objects. The TV was placed as high as possible. Yep, I got that too. A TV set too low is a major accident waiting to happen. I felt at home in the strangest way. This was the first house we'd been to where the same daily struggles were happening. These people had the same ninjalike instincts we did of moving drinks and plates before the Angels could grab and destroy them. They weren't stiff or awkward around Isabella and just laughed and removed her hands when she grabbed hair or glasses. It was second nature for them as it had become for us. We didn't have to continually apologize for our daughter's behavior or hold her arms at constant bay from destroying the house. It was "Angel proof" (as we call it), and we could breathe easy and enjoy ourselves. It was the most comfortable we'd ever been with Isabella in someone else's home. Meeting Dave and Terry Jo Bichell was a good thing.

Terry Jo was involved in Angelman Syndrome research and had studied Angelman kids all over the world. She was amazed and intrigued at how advanced Isabella was.

"She's one of the highest functioning Angels I've ever seen," she told us as we left that evening. For years, we thought we'd been doing everything wrong and blaming ourselves for Isabella's delays. Now we were learning that we'd been helping her more than we knew. She wasn't severely delayed after all. She was high functioning, given her condition. That knowledge alone opened the world up for us and allowed us to breathe as parents. "I'd love to study her more and keep in touch with you guys." After that magical evening, a friendship was formed. We periodically had dinner with the Bichells and went to events together. Louie and Isabella even went on their first date and saw Sesame Street live. Of course, Yolanda, Terry Jo, and I were there to buy popcorn and keep the other children from having their hair pulled. A good time was had by all. We learned from each other and shared information.

We found Terry Jo to be a treasure trove of knowledge. She helped us find doctors who could adjust medications and specialists who could point us in the right direction with therapies, etc. She was intrigued by our self-learned remedies and nutritional approaches.

One night while we were all having dinner, Terry Jo was

asking in-depth questions about Isabella's diet—no refined sugar, no refined flour, no processed foods, no fast food, no soda, etc., etc. She told us of another woman in Chicago who had been doing the same thing with her daughter and who'd been getting great results from it. I immediately asked for the woman's name and if she could get me her number. The next day, I called Paula Evans in Chicago.

I waited until after lunch to make the call. I walked into the living room and dialed the number—another cold call.

"Hello?" the tiny, razor-sharp voice answered.

"Hi, is this Paula Evans?"

"Yes, this is Paula."

"This is Regie Hamm. I'm from Nashville, Tennessee, and I got your number from Terry Jo Bichell. I have a daughter with Angelman Syndrome, and I think we may have some interesting things in common."

I went on to explain the story of the last five years to Paula. I told her about the doctor who'd changed our lives through nutrition and how we had applied those principles to Isabella. According to Terry Jo, Isabella was high functioning, and her daughter was also high functioning. I didn't think that was coincidence. Paula listened without a sound and then began to tell me her story.

Paula lit into the Angelman Syndrome problem with the fervor of a Pentecostal preacher. Her high, Fran Dresher-like, New York accent spit out facts and figures so fast I could hardly keep up. She quoted the science chapter and verse and seemed to have a handle on the disorder and who in the world was studying it, the key scientific players, and where each were in his or her own research. She had a firm grasp on the disorder and a clear passion to get to the bottom of ending it. She was a true believer in nutritional interventions (as were we) and practiced them with her own daughter, Ainsley. Paula was a revelation. I listened to her in absolute amazement. Finally, at the end of her one-hour diatribe, she said, "Regie, what's happening to our kids is unacceptable. I refuse to sit idly by and let it continue. My daughter is trapped inside herself. I want to get her out."

This fired me up, and a huge grin spread across my face. Paula began speaking in rapid-fire phrases. "Ed Weeber cured this in a mouse down in Nashville years ago. I've been in contact with him. He believes a cure is possible. I have him on speed dial, and I'm going to move heaven and earth to get him whatever he needs. Keep in contact with me."

For the next several months, Paula and I exchanged e-mails. Finally, she sent an e-mail that dumbfounded me. She was starting a foundation that would be dedicated to funding the promising research Ed Weeber was doing in the field of Angelman Syndrome. She wanted to create another sanctuary of research for Angelman Syndrome—a complimentary foundation to the Angelman Syndrome Foundation where all approaches—nutritional, scientific, and therapeutic—could be discussed and applied to people with Angelman Syndrome. She wanted to call the foundation FAST (Foundation for Angelman Syndrome Therapeutics), and she wanted me to be the vice chairman of the foundation. I was speechless and humbled. Here I was, a washed-up songwriter and might-have-been pop star with no college education and no real direction for my future. Yolanda and I had only recently received the Angelman diagnosis and were still learning about it. Paula had secured scientists, lawyers, Wall Street executives, and Princeton professors to be on her board. Why on earth would this woman want me there? It was a mystery to me, but it felt like a doorway I needed to enter. Suddenly, my life wasn't just about songs and records and staying afloat. Something more important was at play in my newly expanding world, and I knew that it too was not random and not accidental. I reluctantly agreed to vice chair her board of directors. FAST was born.

THE TIME OF MY LIFE

*W*hile I was walking through the house to my office to scour more jobs on the Internet, Yolanda stopped me and said, "You know, you should really watch this season of *American Idol.* There are some great singers this year. I think you'd dig this David Cook kid. Check him out."

Years ago, Isabella had become obsessed with the bad singers on early *American Idol* episodes. As the season progressed, she would lose interest. But by then, Yolanda was hooked. I had always had professional contempt for the show. Why should some kid get to be a star just because he was on a TV show for thirteen weeks? I'd been slugging it out my whole life. So had many of my brilliant friends. *Idol* was doing such great business; however, it became a thing pros tolerated. If you could get a song on a Carrie Underwood record or write with Kelly Clarkson, all was okay. The *Idol* artists never felt real to me, but they were here to stay, and I, along with many of my contemporaries, made an uneasy peace with the show and its offspring. Yolanda turned up the volume on the TV. Cook was belting out that cool version of Billie Jean I'd always liked.

"Wow. That kid actually has something, huh?" I said, surprisingly impressed. "Who's your favorite?"

"I love this chick from Australia, awesome voice. She used to have a deal, but it all fell apart before it got off the ground. We know that story, huh?"

"Yes, my dear, we do know that story," I said, with a faraway stare. "'Kay. Have fun. I'm down in the office if you need me."

"Hey, Reg. Dude"—Yolanda has always called me dude, and I love that—"they're having that songwriter contest again this year. You know, the thing Scotty won last year?" My dear, long-time friend, Scott Krippayne, had written "This Is My Now" the year earlier and won the songwriting contest. I'd danced around the kitchen in celebration when I saw him on TV. By then I'd forgotten all about it. "Well, they're doing it again, and I totally think you need to write something for it. In fact, I *want* you to!" Yolanda had never asked me to write anything in all our years together. She was serious. "You have nothing going on. You have no publishing deal, no record deal, no anything."

"Wow. Thanks for reminding me, sweetie. That's so sensitive of you!" I joked.

"I'm serious, dude. You know you can write this thing; I know you can write this thing. Just get your butt down there and do it. You have a week, so chop, chop."

"You really want me to go for this?"

"I really, *really* want you to go for this. You have nothing to lose."

"Okay. If I'm going to do it, I need this whole week. I've got that jingle thing I have to do. I'll need all the time I can get, so you'll have the kids full time. You good with that?"

"Oh please! Just get to work!"

I walked back down into the office and closed out of the FedEx application I was in. I'd do it next week, maybe the week after.

The phrase that wouldn't leave me alone was "Taste every moment and live it out loud." I wasn't exactly sure what it meant, but it was haunting. The years had broken me but seasoned my soul. I wanted nothing more than to experience everything I could with my wife, son, and daughter. I had lived in the future; I had lived in the past. I wanted to live in the now. "I know this is the time; this is the time" was next and natural. "To be more than a name" appeared. It was true. I wanted to be more than just a recognizable name now; I wanted to be a father and husband, a human. I also wanted to stop feeling invisible. "Or a face in the crowd" was also true. It was time to live again. "This is the time, this is the time of my life." I had a chorus that night. That was a Thursday.

The following Monday, I blocked the day off and went to work early, around tenish. I called my band, Matt Pierson, Tony Morra, and Ron Robinson, and booked them for a Tuesday tracking session. The song wasn't written yet, but I had to move quickly. If it all fell apart, they would let me cancel without putting up a fuss. The session was booked; I had to write the song. The melody came quickly and instinctively—the way melodies always have for me. I usually know in an hour or so if there's something compelling there. It felt good. It felt natural. I wanted to try something with the parallel minor in the bridge. What developed was unconventional, but I loved it. I didn't think too much about it and went with it. It ended on a high note, and I knew the *Idol* people would probably like that. It was the only self-conscious moment in the writing of that song. Next came the lyrics. They just came out. "I've been waiting on my dreams to turn into something I could believe in" was unexpectedly

221

autobiographical. I hadn't meant to infuse my personal struggles into this puff piece for a song contest, but I was. I went with it and let it flow. "Looking for that magic rainbow on the horizon" actually made perfect sense to me in that moment. Later, that line would stir controversy and get ripped by reviewers, but I felt like I'd been chasing a phantom pot of gold for years. As I understand the mythology, you find those things at the end of rainbows. Were one to actually find said pot of gold, the rainbow that led you there would certainly seem magical. I wasn't then and still am not bothered by that line. I stand by it completely.

Letting go and giving in to love was the essence of what I wanted and needed to say, so I did. Watching the bitterness burn and giving into love is kind of another way of saying, "I surrender all." I found myself rewriting the nemesis hit fifteen years later in a new way with new perspective and with a heart that truly meant the words. In just under three hours, the first verse and chorus were done. I took a break, had lunch with my wife and son, and went back down to the office to finish.

"Holding on to things that vanished into the air left me in pieces" literally came out of my mouth intact. The line caught me off guard, and I choked up. It took an hour or so to collect myself and button up the verse. When I finally got to the heart of what I was talking about, "All that I needed was there all along, within my reach, as close as the beat of my heart," I knew it was complete and true. The ambition and drive I'd thought would save me wasn't what I needed. The talent I thought would carry me wasn't what I needed. What I needed most was the love and truth I'd only seen as obstacles. I knew now that this was all that I needed, and it was closer than I imagined.

The bridge lines wrote themselves. I wanted to face my uncertain future with clean hands and a pure heart and keep my feet on the ground, my arms open wide, my face to the sun. In five hours, I had assembled a song that took literally years to write. I had no idea if any *American Idol* people would like it or want to sing it, but that's what I had to say in that song. It wasn't about conquering or winning or having your time in the spotlight. I'd had that life, and it had failed me. I'd been on the mountain, and it crumbled. I couldn't write something untrue. This was true.

On Tuesday, I tracked the guitars, bass, drums, and over-dubbed the keyboards at my office/studio. On Wednesday, I sang the vocal. Before I had it mixed, I made one slight change. The original track had a dramatic twenty-second intro. I realized upon reading the Web site rules that voters would only be required to listen to thirty seconds of each song. I decided to give them as much actual song as possible, so I edited the intro down to one chord played on the acoustic guitar, four seconds. If I was going to lose this thing, it wasn't going to be because of some self-indulgent intro. I wanted to lose or win on the merits of the song itself. With that done, on Thursday, I gave it to my dear friend and long-time mix engineer, Paul Salveson. Friday morning (the deadline), he posted the mix, and it sounded great. I went to the song contest Web site and entered "The Time of My Life" in the contest, along with my ten-dollar entry fee. I then turned my attention to the Stokes Lighting Center jingle that was due the same day and that I was getting paid five hundred dollars to write, sing, and produce. I was infinitely more excited about the Stokes ad. It was a bird in the hand. The *Idol* thing was a long shot and something fun to try at best. I'd put absolutely no faith in winning the thing. With tens of thousands of entries, the odds were just too slim. I wasn't really convinced they would even hear it with that many entries. Still, Yolanda wanted me to do it, so I did.

Sunday night, I received an e-mail stating that I might be in the top twenty entries. I wasn't to talk about the contest to anyone until those decisions had been made. Easy enough. At that point, I couldn't have cared less about it. It was still pie in the sky. I was waiting on the next lighting store ad. Monday morning, I got another e-mail confirming my song was indeed in the top twenty. Now, I was interested. This was cool. It had been a long time since I was actually in the running for a win as a songwriter. Still, the odds weren't great. I went to the Web site and listened to all the other entries. At the end of it, I felt like I had as good a shot as anyone of winning, but you just never get your hopes up about these things. It's the first rule of songwriting; it's all nothing until it's something. The voting would go on for a month. I had other things to attend to and babies to feed. This was a mild amusement and an interesting distraction. Nothing more.

Contrary to popular belief, Scott Krippayne and I only spoke about the song contest twice. Once, after he won, I congratulated him at dinner one night with two other friends. We all asked some inside baseball questions. "Was it an amazing experience? Did you meet anyone cool? Were there any long-term benefits professionally?" He answered no to all of them, and we moved on to different topics. The other time we talked about it was when I got in the top twenty. He called me to congratulate me and give me one piece of advice: "Dude, don't read the blogs. Just stay away from the blogs. That's all I can tell you."

"Anything else I should know?" I asked, hoping there was some secret handshake I could learn that would give me a leg up.

"Nope. It's pretty much out of your hands how. Love ya, dude. Hope you win. Don't read the blogs. See you later." That was the extent of the grand, *American Idol* songwriting conspiracy—two guys who happened to know each other. That relationship would become maddeningly controversial all too soon.

About halfway through the voting process, I broke the

cardinal rule and went to the blogs to get a feel for which songs were finding favor. As I scrolled and read and tried to figure out if anybody liked my song, I found that the race was between three frontrunners. My song wasn't one of them. In fact, no one was even mentioning "Time of My Life" as a contender. For a second, the sting of yet more invisible failure left me crestfallen. The whole thing had truly passed me by. Maybe I'd always been second- or third-rate talent. Maybe I'd just gotten lucky all those years ago and had a good run ending in a fluke shot at stardom. I breathed in, breathed out. I smiled. It was okay. For the first time, it was really okay. I had my wife and my kids, and we were okay. I exited out of the madness that was the *AI* songwriting contest blogosphere and never went back. I got on with life and forgot about the whole thing. I figured I'd watch from home and be able to say, "Oh yeah, I remember that song. Good for them."

Yolanda had been absolutely certain I would win from the moment she heard the other songs. She wouldn't let it go and insisted we be in "TV shape" by the finale just in case. I figured giving my body a health jolt wasn't a bad idea anyway, so we ordered our vitamins and began the liquid diet that had so radically changed out lives seven years earlier. I had given up on winning, and by the time the Thursday before the finale show rolled around, I was hoping someone would call to confirm the fact that I had indeed lost so I could eat something. I was tired of all this—the song contest, the show, the "David versus David" nonsense. I just wanted it all to be over. I'd said my piece. That was enough for me.

We'd been through a tough three day stretch with Bella. That Thursday I was exhausted and had to take an afternoon nap. Yolanda told me to stay awake in case the Idol people called. "They're not going to call today, baby, and I couldn't care less if they do. I'm dying here. If they call, you talk to them." I crawled under my sheets and slept like a baby without Angelman Syndrome for two hours. It was glorious. When I woke up, Isabella was home from school, and the house was buzzing. I checked my phone to see several messages and then checked the computer to see several e-mails from my contact at the contest. I knew this meant I'd either won or lost. I was truly fine either way.

I cleared my voice, rubbed my recently awakened eyes, and dialed the number. My contact picked up. "Hello, this is Jeff."

"Jeff, this is Regie Hamm," I said, holding back a yawn.

"Regie, hi. You won," he said in the most matter-of-fact way.

"I won? Really? Oh…wow…really?" I was completely dumbfounded.

"Yep, you're the winner. Congrats. Okay, we've got some planning to do, and we don't have much time. You have a *USA Today* interview in twelve hours, and we need to discuss a few things." He was all business. "You're going to be contacted by a publicist who will walk you through some dos and don'ts. Basic stuff like royalty rates for iTunes, how much money you're going to make, etc."

"Okay, well that stuff is easy because I don't know any of those things, and this is the first time we've ever talked about them."

"Second thing is this: your past in the music business is starting to come up. People think you're some kind of hand-picked ringer and that the contest is a scam. We all know that's not true, but you might want to tone down the part of your story where you had a record deal and maybe not lean so heavily in to the hit songs you've written, etc. We're not asking you to lie, but if you could find a way to sidestep talking about that stuff, it would help out. Finally, please don't talk about knowing Scott Krippayne.

For some reason, your friendship with him is sending people off the deep end, and they assume the contest is rigged."

"Okay, Jeff. Well, trust me; there's plenty I can talk about other than my brief time in the spotlight. As far as Scotty goes, if someone asks me point blank if I know him, I'm answering yes. He's been my friend for many years, and I'd never deny that. But you have my word not to bring it up if someone else doesn't. Is that good enough?"

"Good enough. Okay, let's talk plane tickets. You'll be getting a call from our travel agent for one ticket and one hotel room—"

I interrupted, "Hey, Jeff, any chance of getting a ticket for my wife? All the other writers had co-writers. Since I didn't have a co-writer, would you guys be willing to pick up her ticket?"

He paused. "We really don't have that kind of thing in the budget. Do you know anyone you could stay with in LA? If you could take care of your own lodging, we'll pick up her ticket." I stared at the phone. Was the biggest show in the world really asking me this question? Was I really about to cut corners for *American Idol*?

"Uh … I guess … I don't really … well, I do have some family out there, but—"

"So maybe you guys could bunk with some of them?"

"I … sure … I … yeah … okay, well, I guess we'll cover our own lodging then." My sister-in-law lived in a studio apartment and didn't have the room, so I did the math in my head and realized a plane ticket would cost about as much as a hotel room. So it was a wash. Still, this was all about a sum of money less than five hundred dollars. It meant a lot to me right about then, but I really didn't think it would to them. This was such a strange request, but given my grogginess from sleep and the fact that I was still processing the win, I just agreed.

"Great. Okay, we'll get you two tickets to LA then. Your

next phone call should be with the travel agent. Thanks, Regie. Congrats again."

I walked upstairs, through the house, and back into the master bedroom where Yolanda and Isabella were lounging on the bed. "Hey. We won," I said, soft and deliberate. Yolanda squealed in delight and started dancing with Isabella on the bed. Bella squealed in delight in return although she had no idea what was happening. She just knew Mom and Dad were happy about something and that made her happy. It was as tender and lovely a moment as I've ever had in my life. There was precious little time to celebrate, however. We had to make many arrangements in the next three days. Monday we'd be on a flight to LA.

Ed Nash was a young, twenty-something man about town. While I was watching my career end before my very eyes, his was just beginning. We met, by random chance, at a Halloween party I'd been invited to a year after I'd lost my record deal. It was one of those musician parties where all the new up and comers would be hanging out. I was reluctant to show my face, but Yolanda had encouraged me to go and meet some new people, so I went. I sauntered through the crowded house in regular street clothes, sidestepping hipsters in crazy costumes racing for more beer. The only person I knew was the guy who lived there, and I wasn't seeing him. I decided to quietly duck out and head home. This wasn't my scene. Just then, he spotted me, "Regie! Hey, man! You came!"

"Yeah, I thought I'd pop in on you. Thanks for the invite."

"All right. Get downstairs in the studio. You're playing some songs for us right now."

"Aw, man, really? I just stopped in to—"

"Nope, you're doing it. Call it a favor to me. Get down there."

I descended into his basement studio where everyone had now been assembled and I was ushered to the keyboard.

"Everybody, this is one of my favorite writers of all time, Regie Hamm!" was the introduction. I was in the throes of losing everything, but my dad always taught me to play like it's your last time every time. So I did. Three songs and an encore. It was the best gig I'd done all year in front of about twenty fresh-faced cats, witches, and Shreks in a stone basement studio. I thanked everyone for listening, thanked the gracious host, and was heading out. Just as I got to the front door, Ed tapped my arm. "Hey, man, I was blown away by what you did there. I'm starting my own management company and would love to talk to you sometime. What's going on with you?"

"Well, I just lost my record deal and my house. My newly adopted daughter doesn't sleep, and I have no idea what I'm doing with my life. How 'bout you?" He laughed and handed me a card.

"Okay, well if you need someone to help you figure it all out, give me a call. I like those kinds of challenges." I wasn't smiling.

Ed and I ended up having lunch months later, and I spilled the entire story of what had happened to me. He looked across the table and said words I'll never forget. "Wow, dude. Well, that's heavy, and I don't know how you fix this right now, but look, if you need someone to pick up your dry cleaning or take your car to the DMV, let me help you. I don't need to be paid, and you obviously don't need another expense in your life, but I love what you do and would love to help you figure it out. Just call me if you need me." He didn't know it, but he was being the voice of Jesus for me. None of my long-time friends had made that offer. Though I had support from some close family members and a few dear, life-long friends, not many people seemed to recognize the trouble I was in. Ed reached out and asked for nothing in return at a time when I had nothing to give. He went on to be there through all my struggles on Music Row. He ended up booking shows for me and helped me get leads on production projects. Never once did he ask me to sign a contract or pay him anything. Even when it looked like it was completely over, he was still there championing my cause.

Ed's business partner, Tom Rutledge, had also been instrumental in my life. Tom saw me playing with Smokey Lonesome (the southern rock band) the night he and Ed formed their new partnership, Rutledge Nash and Associates. Tom had heard the *American Dreams* project years earlier and had been a fan. Tom had played guitar for the likes of Dolly Parton, Alan Jackson, Faith Hill, Brooks and Dunn, just to name a few. He'd seen all you can see in the music business and possessed a unique perspective I desperately needed. He took me aside after the show and offered what Yolanda called "the best words of wisdom you've heard yet." He said, "Reg, this is a great band, and I get why you're doing this. You're hurting, and this is a Band-Aid for the pain. Sooner or later, you'll stop being a side man, stop drinking whiskey out of the bottle, and get back to being you. That's when everything will turn. Ed and I will be here for you either way. We love you, and we love what you do."

I hadn't experienced that kind of unconditional acceptance in the music business. These guys became like family to me over time, and now they were buckled in to the *American Idol* roller coaster ride with me as well. It just so happened they were going to be in LA representing another client the same days Yolanda and I would be there for the finale. As it turned out, we were all on the same flight. They were staying at the Sportsman's Lodge in Burbank, an understated, out-of-the-way, old-school hotel. Yolanda and I booked a room there as well. Having Ed and Tom there would prove to be priceless.

Arrangements were made. My mother and father would stay at our house and take care of the kids for three days. This was a big deal. We'd never been away from Bella that long since we'd had her. Her routine was stringent and physically demanding. We made copious notes to be followed to the letter regarding medications, what she could and couldn't eat, how to bathe her, when to put her to bed, how to put her to bed, and on and on. Gabe: just a two-year-old who eats sleeps and poops. Easy as pie. We rummaged through our closets to find anything from the past that could be worn on a red carpet. I found a designer shirt I'd had gotten for a photo shoot seven years earlier in the back of my closet. I couldn't afford to buy anything new, so this was it. Yolanda packed the vintage dress she'd worn to our last award show many years earlier. This was the best we could do. We had no money. We knew we'd have expenses on our three-day jaunt, including the inexplicable hotel room expense, so we borrowed two thousand dollars from my sister-in-law. This would cover food, lodging, rental car (*AI* said they'd reimburse me for that), gas, and anything unforeseen—there would be a lot of that.

The correspondence with Paula Evans continued, and the new foundation was coming together. I wasn't sure what I was doing, but I wanted to help. I was still learning and listening and finding out all I could about Angelman Syndrome, meeting everyone I could meet, and getting an education on this disorder and this community. Yolanda, Ed, Tom, and I were to fly to LA on Monday. It just so happened that Doctor Ed Weeber, the premier AS researcher in the country and man who'd cured the Angel mouse, was going to be in town on Sunday night and had no plans for dinner. Paula, being the tenacious connector she is, arranged for Dr. Weeber and I to meet. The conversation would be heavy.

I picked him up at his hotel, and we drove downtown to a

restaurant. I was aching for a salad. We went through the usual paces of dining—hostess, waiter, order, small talk, food, get to the point.

"I think your daughter knows she is how she is," he said, staring through his studious glasses. "I think these kids are as smart as regular kids but are just locked up in their own world as the result of some disconnection process in the brain. What's more, I think we can fix it."

I sat silently while my heart raced and chills raced up my spine. "What do you mean by fix it?" I asked.

"I mean, I think in theory, we could give your little girl a pill on a Wednesday night, and she'd wake up Thursday morning completely normal. Granted, it's just a theory, and we're a long way from it, but it's not out of the realm of possibility. In fact, because we know exactly what causes this, most of my colleagues agree this is probably a relatively simple thing to cure. We need time and money. That's it."

A wave of nausea hit me as I pondered the Pandora's box of my daughter waking up "normal." I had a thousand questions. Would she be able to speak? Would she have memories of being the other way? Would she need therapy to reintroduce her to the world of "normalcy"? Could she relapse? Would she have emotional damage? Would there be behavioral tradeoffs? The questions were racing through my mind at light speed, but I remained silent. This was almost too much to take in. Dr. Weeber continued on with the science. Some of it I understood, most of it I didn't.

"What would finding a cure for this be comparable to? Discovering penicillin? Antibiotics?" I asked. He thought for a moment.

"We're so out on the edge here, I don't think there's a comparison to be made. We're talking about doing something only seen on *Star Trek*, but at it's core, it's relatively simple. We're simply straightening out some confused wiring. If you get glasses, you're just correcting weak ocular transmitters. In a sense, that's what we'd be doing here, just with epic results."

"Final question," I said. "You guys have so many smart people on this board. I dropped out of college my freshman year. Why do you need a stupid songwriter on this board?"

"Well," he said with a sly grin, "to be honest, we don't really know. We just know a stupid songwriter is exactly what we need."

At that point, no one except my parents knew I'd won the contest. This foundation wasn't looking for some sort of cheap, temporary, tabloid newsmaker. They saw some value in me I hadn't being seeing for years now. That week, I had held the first annual "Bella Bash" fundraiser and had donated the proceeds to the Angelman Syndrome Foundation. The director of that foundation had been in contact with me and been talking to me about future efforts. Now, this new foundation was actually asking me to sit on their board. Somehow the entire Angelman Syndrome community was coming to my rescue in ways they couldn't have known. I was starting to believe less and less in random things.

THE MAGIC RAINBOW

My father was taking Yolanda and me to the airport. He had just come from a funeral, a very special funeral. Dottie Rambo had been a songwriting hero of mine. Her family group, The Rambos, were gospel music royalty by the time I was old enough to listen to music. When I was a child, my family actually opened for the Rambos once in Atlanta. Dottie and her music were permanently ingrained in my soul. She was part of that past with which I continually did battle. Dottie had been killed in a tragic bus accident five days before I was to get on a jet for LA and the biggest television music event of the year. Her memorial service just happened to be the day we left—random. Dad showed up to take us to the airport still in his suit and carrying the program from her memorial service. As we packed the van, did the final house check, kissed the kids, and saddled up for the trip to BNA, he told us about the service, and we all began to get a little weepy recounting her music and influence. As we drove, I stared at her picture on the front of the program and then flipped it over to read the timeless words of her classic song, "We

Shall Behold Him."

"Can I keep this, Dad?" I asked, choking back tears.

"Sure, son, take it with you. You okay?"

"Yeah, just a heavy week, you know?"

He looked at me with a warm, fatherly smile. "I know, buddy, I know." For a brief moment, I was ten years old again. The pain of the recent years subsided , and the eternal things I'd been raised to know were comforting. Even now, as I was about to go back to the world of pop culture and this time as a conquering hero, the music of my childhood and the truth my father had proclaimed his entire life was surrounding me and holding me in its warm embrace. There was nothing random about this program I held in my hand. Once again, irony and circumstance were the voice of God to me, and it was whispering, "Don't lose your perspective this time. This is all fleeting vanity. Enjoy yourself, but don't believe in it." I kept Dottie's picture in my songwriting notebook, which I still carry everywhere, and looked at it every day of the trip.

Yolanda and I hadn't been on a plane together in almost five years. It would be nice staring at the clouds with her again. We stood in the baggage line together for the first time in what seemed like a lifetime. We casually strolled through the terminal, into the jet bridge, and down to our seats. We belted in and waited on movement, sweet movement. We smiled at one another as we felt the familiar speed change to lift and finally, to wheels up. Next stop: LA.

I had no idea what to expect in these two days. I'd actually never watched an entire *American Idol* finale show. I'd briefly seen Scott Krippayne on the previous year's show only because one of our mutual friends called and yelled, "Turn on *American Idol* right now! Scotty won the songwriting contest and is on right now! 'Kay. Bye!" We had turned the finale show on just in time to watch Scott stand next to Ryan Seacrest, smile, and wave. We raised a toast to him, listened to Jordin Sparks sing his song, and went on about the evening. I assumed I'd get some briefing on what to expect soon enough. We landed, rented the car, drove to the hotel, checked in, and called Jeff, my contest contact. He gave us directions to the 19 offices—the production company that produces *American Idol*—and told us to come by and get our tickets. We dove into the LA chaos toward Hollywood.

Through the traffic, we spotted the building, miraculously found parking, and headed past security, up the elevator to the receptionist. "Hi, I'm Regie Hamm. Here to see Jeff King."

"Yes, Mr. Hamm, he's expecting you. I'll get him. Would you like anything?"

"No, thank you."

Jeff arrived with another hip, thin, LA music biz associate. They both congratulated Yolanda and me profusely and were incredibly nice and accommodating. Jeff asked Yolanda if he could pull me aside for a moment. She talked to his friend while he spoke privately with me in hushed tones.

"Regie, I want you to know between us that you won this thing fair and square. I know you know a lot of people in the music business, and some of them have connections to 19, but you were eligible to enter this contest by the letter of its guidelines; you entered through the Web site like everybody else and won handily with more votes than anyone else. I just wanted to tell you that with no one else around so you can always sleep easy knowing this." Sleep easy? He obviously didn't know Isabella. He then went on to give me the names of the people who had reviewed my song and passed it on through the channels. Apparently, the top twenty contenders had been narrowed down through a legion of A&R listeners and then sent to Simon Fuller himself for final selection. Once the top twenty was posted, it was all based on voting. "One more thing, Reg. I know we've talked about this, but the Scott Krippayne thing has gotten completely out of control." I had no idea what he was talking about. I hadn't been following this on the Internet, but according to him, the Scott-Regie connection and conspiracy was a wildfire. "There are people who want to file lawsuits and everything you can think of."

"Really?" I asked, completely taken aback. "Over a song contest? Why?"

"My friend, I've discovered that songwriters are crazy. You're the sanest one I've dealt with yet." He obviously didn't know me very well. I wasn't acting crazy to him because I wasn't holding on that tightly to this. It had simply been a request from my wife that I honored. I had been honest in my song. I had made peace with disappointment and heartbreak. This was just a fun night out for my me and my wife, nothing more.

"Okay, well, again, I won't bring him up unless I'm asked about him. That's all I can really commit to. I think this is all kind of ridiculous. He is my friend."

"Just keep it in mind while you're doing interviews. That's all we ask."

"Speaking of all that stuff, what is my itinerary for the next couple of days?" I had been given no information to that point.

"A publicist will be in touch with you about doing some press, and we've got show tickets for you and your wife to both shows."

"Am I going to be on camera? Do you have an idea of what I should expect? Just trying to get my arms around all this."

"I think they are working on a camera shot for you. I'll be in touch the whole time as well as the publicist. You'll have information coming as we get it." I said okay, and we left. That was the last time I saw him. On the way back to the hotel, the publicist called.

"Regie?"

"This is Regie," I replied.

"Hi, this is—" I can't remember her name. We had one two-minute conversation. "—with the PR firm handling the finale show."

"Yes, how are you? Do you have an itinerary for me?" I sort of yelled into the flip phone as the LA traffic buzzed around me.

"Regie, we've finished all the press for today, so nothing today. You'll do some of the shows in the morning, and then I think we're going to forgo having you on the red carpet tomorrow night. I just don't want to throw you in that shark tank." I kind of looked at the phone and scowled in disbelief.

"Well, if it helps, I've sort of done this before. I know I'm not really supposed to talk about it, but I'm okay with all this stuff. It's not going to freak me out or anything."

"Yeah, I think we'll just forego. Listen, have fun tomorrow and congratulations!" Click. *What just happened?* I thought to myself. *I thought winning this thing was supposed to be about the experience, blah, blah, blah.* My wife had been changing diapers and getting up before dawn and sitting in hospital rooms with a seizing infant and wearing her body and mind down with no help from anyone except me for the last five years. She'd been through hell and back yet still had enough faith in me to ask me to write a song for this stupid show. She hadn't gotten dressed up for a night out like this in years. She wanted to walk the red carpet and do the whole deal. I wasn't going to let this slide.

We went back to the hotel and went up to Ed's room where he had set up a command center of computers, printers, BlackBerries, files, and an open briefcase full of information. He and Tom were working for another client but were obviously excited and interested in what was transpiring with the show. "Dude, they're not giving me a publicist for the red carpet. The chick in charge booted it. She said she didn't want to throw me in the shark tank." We laughed hysterically.

"Yep, she booted it. With all these VIPs running around, she probably can't spare an extra body to put on you, so she let you down easy," he said in a cool and relaxed way. "I can handle you on the carpet if they'll let me."

"Let me e-mail Jeff and see."

I e-mailed Jeff at 19 and made a plea for Ed to be my publicist on the red carpet. I explained how he'd done it many times before, understood half sheets—an information card about half the size of a sheet of paper that gives the bullet points and vital statistics of the artist—and prepping the line—when the publicist walks in front of an artist from reporter to reporter explaining who he is, what he's doing there, how to spell his name correctly, and handing out half sheets—and could totally be trusted to make it all happen in the most professional way possible. Jeff agreed to it. Ed and Tom dropped what they were doing and went to work on the half sheets.

The first finale show was Tuesday. We knew this day would not be the crazy one. No red carpets, no limos—just spectators tonight. The one piece of drama that did give us a temporary jolt was Yolanda losing the show tickets. For about two hours, the sky was falling. I contacted Jeff about the possibility of getting new ones printed. I might as well have been asking him to fetch a Faberge egg from the mouth of a unicorn. Apparently, *American Idol* finale tickets are a big deal and really hard to come by. I was fascinated by all this hype. Why was everything about this show such a big deal to people? Believe it or not, a maid turned the tickets in to lost and found. To me, that's still the most amazing part of the whole story. She could've gotten a thousand dollars a piece for them, but she turned them in. God bless her. Crisis averted.

Yolanda and I drove our rented convertible to the Nokia Theater. For some reason, the top wouldn't come down. Oh well, no biggie, I guess. We weren't provided with parking passes or credentials of any kind. We just sort of followed the herd to the open doors after paying twenty bucks to park. Our cell phones were confiscated at the door, so I had no way of calling my contact. Was I involved in the show tonight? I had no idea and no information. We found our seat: double E, toward the back.

"I'm sure I'm not featured anywhere tonight with these seats. Cool. We'll just enjoy the show," I said, sort of relieved. We sat and watched the mass of humanity find their seats with their handmade David Cook or David Archuletta posters in full bloom. This was such an interesting curiosity to me. America had only known these two kids for a few weeks, and yet they were deeply emotionally involved in their lives and futures. It was unsettling.

The lights went down. There was nervous applause, and there were involuntary screams rising above shushes. Suddenly, one lone spotlight hit Ryan Seacrest. "This is your American Idol!" The familiar, iconic music bed rose, and the show was underway. There was the obligatory pomposity and ominous advice from Simon, the nondescript wisdom of Randy, and the meandering musings of Paula. Production segments placed the Davids in a heavyweight title fight of sorts. The night would essentially be a sing-off with the winner being catapulted into the stratosphere of the entertainment planet. The stakes of the evening were apparent, even to a crusty cynic like me. I've never said this publicly, but secretly I was rooting for David Cook. I have nothing against Mr. Archuleta; he seems like a good kid, very talented, very nice. Cook just seemed to possess the life story that would make my song ring true. No seventeen-year-old would give weight to those lyrics. I thought it would be cool for Cook to win, but as the night progressed, I started losing hope for him. The crowd was clearly behind the youngster. Whenever he walked on stage, deafening screams filled the air around us. He was already a superstar.

Toward the end of the show, each of the finalists sang songs he had picked from the contest songs in the top twenty that didn't win. I was curious about this moment. Before each performance, Ryan Seacrest announced the name of the song picked and the names of all the writers of that song. Songwriters are often overlooked and treated as second-class citizens of the music community, and I thought it was cool to honor them like this. I also thought to myself, *Wow, if they're being this cool to the guys who didn't win, I can only imagine how cool my night will be tomorrow. This is great.* Once again, the optimist in me wanted to believe.

The day started at 5:00 a.m. I was up and in the shower, clothes pressed and on the door. I shaved, brushed, coiffed, splashed, dressed, and was out the door to meet Ed by six. We had to be at the press pavilion by seven. As Ed drove us through the dark, LA morning, I got a cell phone call from an unknown number. Any call this early must be an emergency. With Bella, you never know. I answered.

"Regie baby!" I recognized the voice immediately. It was Dave Wingert, a radio personality I'd met in Seattle all those years ago. He'd given *American Dreams* great marks and had added "Babies" to his syndicated show. He was flamboyant and quite frankly the only man alive who ever called me "Regie baby." He was a good memory from better days.

"Dave?" I said, slyly drawing it out.

"You remember? Regie baby, how are you? I just read the news in *USA Today*, and I'm just so happy for you! Can we talk on the air?"

"Fire it up, Dave. I'm ready." I was back in the zone for a

minute. My instincts were returning, and I was re-experiencing what it was to be liked again. I won't lie; it felt good.

As the eastern sun melted west and awakened the city of angels, Ed and I arrived at the pavilion. We once again realized we had no credentials or parking passes. After parking blocks away and then standing like tourists at the security gate being staved off by the completely unimpressed security guard, our publicist casually sauntered up. She still had sleep lines on her bare face and was wearing jeans, a sweatshirt, and flip flops, just-out-of-bed wear. As she walked us from camera to camera, she yawned and texted and looked for comfortable places to sit. This was clearly an imposition to her, and she was letting Ed do most of the work. In her defense, I'm sure handling the songwriting contest winner at dawn is the worst PR duty you can pull in Tinseltown. After telling the story of how and why I wrote the song and dodging the "who would you rather hear sing your song" question for three straight hours, it was over. It was almost eleven, and the LA haze was burning off. "Looks like another perfect day…"

Yolanda was racing around to find a place to get her makeup done. We couldn't afford the services who came to the hotel, so she went to the MAC store and had them do it for fifty bucks. I wanted to get a run and a nap in before the show. No dice. Too many interviews, too much to arrange. I kept calling Jeff, my contact at 19, to find out what I should expect, but I never heard back from him. I wanted to make the night special for Yolanda, so I had the hotel order us a limo. You just can't show up to a red carpet event in a Camry. In hindsight, I wish we had. The concierge assured us it would be covered in our hotel bill. Things were working out. The limo would pick us up at four. We'd be on the red carpet by five. The show started at six, and by eight, one of the Davids would croon my words and music. Perfect.

Yolanda rushed into the room. Her airbrushed face was beautiful and glamorous. Once in the vintage dress, she looked like an old-school movie star from the thirties or forties. This was fun. I donned the ill-fated pirate shirt everyone kept telling me was working. I didn't care; I just wanted to have fun. The limo arrived. Good times ahead. The driver helped Yolanda in, and just before I stepped in, he said, "Oh, sir, uh, I think there's been a misunderstanding of some kind. The hotel didn't add this to their bill somehow. I'll need cash before we leave."

"Cash?" How much cash?" I asked, slightly embarrassed.

"Two hundred and eighty dollars." This was one expensive drive downtown.

"Okay, well, I don't have that much on me. Is there an ATM close?"

"Yes, sir. Right around the corner."

"Okay, take me over there." He pulled up to a convenient store. The portable ATM machine inside would only let me retrieve a hundred bucks at a time. So there I stood like a high school senior going to the prom, reinserting my card three times to extract enough cash to get to the venue. As I nodded at incoming customers who were staring blankly at me in my pirate shirt, trying to get enough cash together to pay the limo driver who was taking me, an official *American Idol* winner, to the most-watched TV show on planet earth, I kept thinking to myself in my best radio voice, *Third caller wins tickets to the* AI *finale show tonight! We'll pick you up in a limo stocked with champagne and chocolate and drive you and four of your closest friends, to the show.* Another hundred bucks. *All you have to do is be the third caller and the limo, champagne, chocolate, and photo ops with the Idols, all on us. Keep it tuned in to this station and be the third caller.* Another hundred bucks. Maybe I would've been better off to win a radio call-in contest.

"Okay, then. I guess we're good to go," I said to the driver in a slightly confused tone as I handed him the wad of twenty dollar bills. I wouldn't let this hamper the evening. Let's go have fun!

The limo rolled through the downtown traffic and finally pulled up to the Nokia Theater. A small crowd of fans cheered and waved signs as we emerged. They had no idea who we were. Ed had been there already and was prepping the line. The mechanical clicking of cameras was everywhere. Chaos was brewing, and with every limo that pulled up, it escalated. Once again, I fielded the "how and why did you write this song" questions and the increasingly intense, "Who do you want to hear sing your song tonight?" My answer was always the same: "David of course." I made the rounds and remembered all over again what I did and didn't miss about success. The journalists (and I use the term describing entertainment reporters loosely) were all respectful and nice. The bigger the star behind me, the quicker the interview so they could get to the red meat. Finally, after an awkward exchange with Jimmy Kimmel's freakish correspondent who laughingly asked me who I was wearing—that was actually funny—it was over, and we were ushered into the theater. I still hadn't heard from my contact. I had no idea what, if anything, I was supposed to do. Upon entering, my cell phone was confiscated yet again. Now I would have no contact with him the rest of the night.

Yolanda and I stood in the lobby in our red carpet clothes, unsure of what to do, while people gawked and speculated as to who we were. We hadn't eaten all day. We were hot and tired and hungry. This had been a strange experience so far, to say the least. We got in line for something to drink. The guy in front of us struck up the conversation as to who we were and why he'd seen us on the red carpet. When I explained who I was and why I was there, he immediately insisted on buying us both a beer. "No, man, really, you don't have to." There it was right in front of me. I was so thirsty, I just chugged it. Chugging a beer on an empty stomach makes one a little loopy. We pulled out our tickets and realized we were in the same bad seats we had been in the night before. My loopy state made me belligerent. "You know what? I'm the only guy who's actually won anything around here yet!" I sort of half-yelled at Yolanda, trying to focus. "I'm tired of not feeling like a winner. I'm going down there and getting good seats for us. Stay here, baby. I'll be back!" I stormed down the aisle, through the pressing crowd, and approached the first person I could find with a clipboard and headset.

"Excuse me, ma'am. I don't know if this matters to anyone, but I'm the songwriting winner. Whoever wins tonight will be singing my song. I'm back in double E. Do I have a camera shot scheduled?" I blurted to the official-looking lady.

"What's your name, sir?"

"Regie Hamm."

"Do you have your ID?"

"Yes, ma'am, right here."

She looked at my ID and ran her fingers down the clipboard. Her eyes got big, and she raised her head. "Oh my gosh. Where did you say you were?"

"Double E. Back there."

"Okay, go back there and sit down. I'll be back to get you in a moment. You're in the wrong place. They do have you scheduled for a camera shot."

I walked back to Yolanda, and we waited. After about ten minutes, the official-looking lady came to get Yolanda and me and walked us to the front row, right next to Ruben Studdard. Had I not said anything, these primo seats would have been filled by seat fillers. I was now ready for the close-up. The lights went down, and the screams, gasps, and shushes flooded the air.

Enter Ryan Seacrest under the spotlight. "This is your American Idol!" Away it went. A- to D-list celebrities were walking up and down the aisles during commercial breaks, girls making sure all their physical attributes were on display in just the right light, guys being cool and coy for the possible camera hit. Mike Myers, Bryan Adams, ZZ Top, Seal, Carrie Underwood, One Republic, and George Michael—all doing business on TV's biggest stage. It was quite a spectacle to watch up close and in person. I befriended a lady sitting next to me, and we got acquainted throughout the show. We would talk during commercial breaks, and she became fascinated with my story and why I was there. As the show progressed, she would look over at me and mouth the question, "Now you think?" She was becoming obsessed with when someone might be bringing up the songwriting contest, the winner, and the winning song. As time dwindled, I must confess I was kind of wondering the same thing. Since I couldn't call my contact, I really had no idea when or if I'd be shown, talked about, mentioned, acknowledged, or ignored. The latter was starting to be the best bet. After sitting through several up-with-people type numbers that took the top ten finalists and shoehorned them into awkward, high-school-drama-club, sing-and-dance routines that looked like warmed-up retreads of the Donnie and Marie show and watching superstars pander to thirty million viewers by doing duets with thirteen-week veterans and watching the white feather suit guy get six complete minutes with the USC marching band, earning him just as much money for the performance of his considered-to-be-a joke song as I was making for the performance of my winning song, I then realized we were in the final fifteen minutes. It was now or never. Finally, it was time for the last song before the big winning announcement. George Michael walked out on to the stage and began. I looked at my watch after the first verse and chorus, he'd been singing for six minutes. He lunged into the second verse of a dirge that was grinding the show to a halt. I said in Yolanda's ear, "You mean there's a second verse to this thing?" Finally, mercifully, he was done. I checked the watch, seven minutes 'til the end of the show. At the last commercial break, the lady sitting next to me was beside herself. "Why haven't they mentioned you yet? Are they really going to sing your song? You think they changed their minds?" I was actually starting to wonder about all those things myself. Surely they hadn't booted it from the show. Could they do that? There wasn't enough time left to get through the whole thing. I knew enough about getting paid from TV performances to know I needed about a minute's worth of airtime to get paid for the prime time performance. At this point, the hotel, Rent-a-Car, limo, red carpet snafu, the not having credentials, parking passes, or good seats meant nothing to me. I just wanted to be mentioned and have a minute of the song aired.

Seacrest: "And we're back." Two minutes left. Ryan went through the drama of the Davids, playing it up to the absolute hilt and the absolute last second. "Your next American Idol is David C—live feed cut—ook!" The place went insane—confetti falling, people screaming and applauding. The noise was deafening. Seacrest buzzed through the next sentence so fast I hardly heard him. "Now here to perform the winning song, 'The Time of My Life,' David Cook!" David jumped in to the tune and sang it all around the stage as his family members wept, and his season mates joined him, finishing with the high G—something I never did in the demo or any other time in my vocal career—standing on the judges' table. There were thirty million people watching and eight thousand people in the Nokia Theater; I was mouthing the words with a thousand-yard stare. I wanted to tell everyone I had written it. They were swaying and lifting their hands and responding to the song, and yet no one in the world knew who the writer of it was. I wasn't sure what this kind of moment was supposed to feel like, but after being passed around as sort of a secondhand winner for two days and in the end not even having my name mentioned when the other writers had been honored the night before felt like a gut punch. I thought this moment might be somewhat redemptive for me after the five years I'd had, but really, all I could see was my sweet mother, an accomplished songwriter in her own right, who had written my first songs with me as a child, who had nurtured my talent and sacrificed her dreams for mine, who had told all her friends about this song and this night, who was, at that very moment, on my couch in my house, tending to my special needs daughter so I could be at this event, looking at my dad and saying, "Ron, did they say his name? Why didn't they mention Regie?" I wasn't angry for myself; I was getting kind of used to this sort of thing, but my mom didn't get to hear my name on *American Idol* after I'd won it. I would later learn that Jeff (my 19 contact) had been imprisoned by an edict to get George Michael's song uploaded to iTunes—a process that normally takes three weeks—by the time he was finished singing, which felt like three weeks. No one could reach him all day because he had been on the phone with Steve Jobs's assistant for ten hours straight. His hands were tied, and I had once again fallen through the cracks of the shifting ground that is the music business.

The confetti had all fallen, and the lights were up. Yolanda and I just stared at the stage. She looked at me and just said, "Baby, what in the world?" The lady who'd been so engrossed in my story took my arm. I looked down at her, and she squinted her eyes at me and said, "What just happened to you?"

"Ma'am, I have no idea," I replied, throwing a smile.

David Cook was still being jerked around the stage by handlers and photographers. Yolanda said, "Dude, you've at least got to go try and meet him." The stage was surrounded by security standing shoulder to shoulder.

"Yeah, okay, I'll try." I walked up to one of the guards and said, "Look, man, I wrote the song that guy just sang, and I would just love to get ten seconds to say hi and congratulate him."

"Where's your credentials? Everybody has to have credentials to get on this stage." He was a very large man, and I was being as nice as possible.

"I know, I know. They have my phone, so I can't call my contact at 19, but I won the songwriting contest. I just don't, that is to say, I wasn't provided . . . there's a woman around here with a clipboard who . . . aw, man, can you cut me some slack on this one? Here's my driver's license."

"You want on this stage, you have to have credentials."

"Okay, look." I had an idea. "There are only two people in this room who know the words to that song he just sang. Me and him. I wrote them." I started quoting the first verse and then broke into the chorus. The security girl standing next to the man said, "Come on, dude, he wrote the song; give him a few seconds." The man took me by the arm and said sternly, "You got thirty seconds." Then he walked me up like a prisoner, never letting go of my arm.

David was about to walk past me. I reached out and grabbed his sleeve. "Hey, man. I'm Regie Hamm. I wrote 'Time of My Life.'" He embraced me, and I could feel him still shaking from the shock. He looked at me and said, "Bro, I just want to tell you—" Just then, he was whisked off the stage and faded to black. There I was, alone on the stage with confetti in my hair.

"Okay, dude, you had your thirty seconds. Let's go." I turned and looked at the thousands of people filing out of the Nokia Theater. I stared at the confetti on the ground as I crunched it under my feet. I felt like I was being walked back to the slammer.

Yolanda and I slowly strolled out of the theater, not really knowing what to do next. We had no passes to any after parties and no instructions. We just stared at each other. "Now what?" she said.

"Maybe Ed has some info for us. Let's go." I stopped off in the bathroom on the way out. While waiting in line for a urinal, I heard one guy yell over to one of his friends, "Hey, man, what about that last song Cook sang? That thing is awesome." Other strangers joined in the chorus. "I loved it too. Yeah, man, cool tune." I just stared straight ahead.

We walked out into the cool air over to the press pavilion. Ruminating on what had just happened had tweaked my angry streak. I was visibly unhappy and walking with a mad tiger gait. I wanted to fight. "Baby, you have to be cool with the press. They don't know all this inside stuff. Reg, settle, baby, settle," Yolanda kept saying, but that just made me angrier.

I snapped at her. "I'm not going to stop being me just because the freaking circus is in town! We haven't been treated professionally. What just happened in there? Why did we even come out here? We could have been home with our kids tonight, not spending borrowed money, watching something else!" I felt slighted. Even as a winner in the rarified air of the largest viewing audience on TV, I was still being humbled. I did some interviews while Ed and Yolanda scrounged for after-party passes.

"Why didn't they acknowledge you tonight, Regie?" was the first question from the first microphone in my face.

"You'll have to ask them. I don't produce the show," I answered, truculent and terse and visibly bothered. It was my standard answer to that question for the next hour.

Ed came over and said, "Finish up this last one. I think I've got us in." I was happy to be done.

Somehow, he'd scared up one pass to the Fox after party, along with a name. The three of us walked over to the party. Ed walked in with his pass while Yolanda and I waited behind the silly velvet rope. Ed found the key person inside and had them come out and walk us all in together. Once again, Ed had saved the day.

The party was one of those where the food's too small and the music's too loud. All the wannabe stars were trying to be seen. All the real stars were trying to be seen trying not to be seen. The white feather suit guy had his own booth and was having picture after picture snapped with children and tipsy fans, reminding me that none of this was about art or even music really. This was about finding something people would stare at long enough to sell air and commercial time. That's what it was always about. It's a TV show. Ed, Yolanda, and I walked, smiled, and took in the sights and sounds like we were at a hi-tech county fair. If you don't know anyone at a party like that and aren't being introduced to people, there are only so many times you can circle the place. Finally, we looked at each other and said, "Let's bail." My *American Idol* experience was officially over.

We plugged the closest In-N-Out Burger into the GPS and followed the British lady's voice through the LA traffic. While I was complaining about the inexplicable night's occurrences and holding my own personal pity party for the way I'd been treated, Yolanda got a text from one of our friends in Nashville. Steven Curtis Chapman's little girl had just been accidentally killed. Suddenly I was sick and ashamed of myself. His precious Maria was not only the same age as my Isabella but also from China. I'd met Steven a couple of times when I was working in CCM, and I knew him to be an amazing man and devoted father. My night had been frustrating, but his night would be hellish. Mine would make for an amusing kitchen table story one day, but his would linger for the rest of his life and change the lives of everyone in his family forever. I shut my impish mouth and stared out the window for the rest of the drive. The thought of what that man and his family were going through at that moment made my head pound. This was far too deep and wide to just be a lesson for me. It was one of those moments that reminded me of what my father had said to me from time to time: "Everything's not about you." This solemn, confusing, heartbreaking event slapped me back to reality, and I could only offer silent prayers for Steven, Marybeth, and their children. I still do today.

After we blotted our tears and collected ourselves, we decided to sit by the pool at the Sportsman's Lodge, eat the burgers, and toast our awkward little evening. We wanted to end the night on a positive note. Yolanda and I walked into the room and discovered that SESAC (my performance rights organization) had sent us some cookies and a bottle of champagne. We changed into sweat pants and T-shirts and converged—Tom, his wife, Sonya, Ed, Yolanda, and I—by the pool of the hotel under the midnight moon. We were the only people there. As we opened the bottle of bubbly, filled glasses, and raised our toast, I looked around the table at the people who were there. I realized their company was the finest I'd been around all week. My wife's striking beauty was stronger than any nipped, tucked, and chiseled would-be starlet on parade. I thought about the picture of Dottie in my notebook and the songs she had written. I thought about Steven Curtis Chapman and his family. Suddenly, the act of surrender made sense to me for the first time in my life. I started to weep while everyone looked at me in bewilderment. The pieces of complete surrender had fallen into place. I realized that God had never actually asked me to surrender anything. My view of surrender had been one of my own making, rooted in my own tainted misunderstanding of what God is and what he asks. In the cool, California air, fumbling through cheeseburgers and sipping carbonated wine, the realization of what God is and what surrendering to him actually means fell on me. God is love. Surrendering to God simply means surrendering to love. God wasn't trying to crush my dreams or rob me of a career. He simply wanted those dreams to be more beautiful and more fulfilling than I could've ever imagined by having them rooted in and growing from a place of love, not just raw ambition and self-focus. The night I had just experienced meant nothing in the eternal light of truth. The five years I had experienced weren't the bad years at all but an exquisite gift, the gift of having a close relationship with my daughter. I'd been allowed to rediscover my wife and new places of strength and beauty I'd never seen in her before. I'd been given a son who would not only carry on my name but who would reintroduce me to the absolute joy of life. I'd been given the chance to work with people who accepted me unconditionally whether I was successful or not. I'd been allowed to view the pinnacle of the entertainment mountain and see it for what it was: dust. I'd been given the ultimate second chance at my dream and finally discovered it to be vanity and vapor.

Dottie and her songs of the eternal played over and over in my mind. I could see her smiling at me in the picture and saying, "You shall behold him, child. Just keep looking." The faces of those who loved me were a revelation staring back at me. Surrender wasn't some deal with God to become a missionary in a mud hut thousands of miles away. It wasn't a promise to not have fun in your life. It wasn't relinquishing your goals and dreams like some third grader caught stealing cookies before dinner. It wasn't a candle-lit commitment ceremony at a church under the watchful eye of a pastor. It was the acknowledgement of something higher and more beautiful than anything I could create or imagine. It was the acceptance of love and truth and knowing that everything good and perfect and worthwhile originated there. It was the faith that everything was going to be all right no matter if my plans worked or not. It was about giving total control to that all-enveloping love and reflecting it back out to the rest of the world. The riddles I'd heard all my life were suddenly being solved in my heart. "Seek ye first the kingdom of God and his righteousness, and all these things shall be added unto you" (Matthew 6:33, KJV). "Whosoever will lose his life for my sake shall find it" (Matthew 16:25b, KJV). In that tender hour, around the still water of a hotel swimming pool, after having been at the most-watched television music event of the year, I finally, willfully, tearfully, and ultimately surrendered all.

FULL CIRCLE

*T*he fact that the *American Idol* finale had run long and cut off on everyone's DVR recording of it turned out to be a good thing. Thousands of people were going to iTunes to find out who won and to download the winning song. In the next four days, there would be over 236,000 downloads of "Time of My Life." There was so much traffic that the iTunes server crashed. As far as I know, that's the only time in the history of iTunes that's ever happened. Where there are usually around one to two hundred comments on a new single, there were over 1,100 comments on this one in the first twenty-four hours of its release. The outpouring of support for David Cook and his unlikely win was a phenomenon. In the middle of that phenomenon, an obscure, washed up songwriter was finding healing in so many ways. The following week, the song entered the Hot 100 at number three. It would reach the number one spot and hover in the top five for weeks to come. In less than a month, it was at the top of the ringtone charts, a place I didn't even know existed. It had been years since I had seen the top of the charts. This time was sweeter than all the others because I knew when people heard this song, they were hearing love. That's all that mattered to me anymore.

The weeks and months that followed found me in new directions. The Angelman Syndrome community became much of my focus. These people had become special and important to me, and I knew that they were not in my life by accident. If I was going to focus on anything now, it would be on things that mattered, not things that didn't. I was told by many of my music business friends how I should spend more time in LA and write with everyone I could get in a room with and parlay this burgeoning success into more success. But nothing was further from my mind. I'd lived that life already. I wanted to be with my family as much as possible. If I could continue to earn a living in music and make my art without becoming an absentee husband and father, that would be wonderful. If I couldn't, I would do something else; that would be wonderful too.

The downloads kept happening—three hundred thousand, four hundred thousand, five hundred thousand, six hundred thousand, seven hundred thousand. I couldn't turn on the TV without hearing David Cook croon "Time of My Life" under some production piece or NBA finals bumper or some finale to some other TV show. I heard it at the grocery store and at the gym and saw David on every morning and late night show from coast to coast. I was being asked to come on various shows as well to tell the story and sing the song. Standing in an aisle at Home Depot one early morning, I heard an employee passing by singing it under his breath. Apparently, this song was not only becoming a hit but being burned into the public consciousness. It was climbing three different radio charts and about to top two of them. Everything a songwriter hopes for from of a song was happening with this one. You can't ask for more than that. I was ecstatic and humbly grateful. The impact of the song had already exceeded all my expectations. This little taken chance, this small step forward had turned into so much more than I would've ever allowed myself to imagine. But then…

On the eighth day of the eighth month of the eighth year of the new millennium, I was downstairs working in my office when suddenly the door was frantically jerked open. "Dude, get up here fast!" Yolanda yelled in what sounded like a panic. Normally, when that tone was used, it meant Isabella was having a seizure or a fever spike. I dropped what I was doing and bolted up the stairs. The television was frozen on Yao Ming's face. "Okay, just watch. I had to run this back so you could see this. I don't even know what to say here." Yolanda pushed the button on the DVR that released the live action. Yao Ming (the famous, seven-foot-plus Chinese basketball star) was holding a small Chinese boy, and they were talking to some reporter about the young boy's hero-ism during that country's recent earthquake disaster. This was obviously the opening ceremonies of the 2008 Olympic games in Beijing, the place Yolanda and I had vowed to be, along with three other families, five years earlier. The ceremonies were end-ing, and the interview with Yao was the final one of the night. Yao is significant because he's from the exact same rural province in China as Isabella. The irony of that certainly wasn't random. As the interviewer tossed the closing remarks to Bob Costas, I could feel what was coming but couldn't believe it.

"From all of us here in Beijing, this is Bob Costas saying good night." The second those words had dissipated into the ether, the four-second guitar intro strummed through my speakers, and it began. David's mellifluous tones spoke the words I'd written a mere five months earlier, just feet away. The sights and sounds of Beijing faded one into the next as he told our story, line by line, to a billion people. The Chinese landscape and culture flashed across the screen while the song one of it's own inspired wafted into the ears of people all over the globe. As David crescendoed into the chorus, a shot of hundreds of little Chinese girls doing tai chi flashed on the screen, and he belted, "Taste every moment and live it out loud." Those little girls weren't much older than my porcelain daughter sleeping in the next room. "Time of My Life" was closing the opening ceremonies of the 2008 Olympic Games in Beijing. I stared dumbfounded and amazed. Yolanda was shaking her hands and sobbing.

"I don't know what to do. I can't handle this," she said through her tears. I gazed at the screen and tried to get a handle on the moment. We couldn't be at the games, but the song was there. The story of our journey was there. Millions of people were hearing the words that had been inspired by a Chinese orphan. Those words were being broadcast from the place Yolanda and I had chosen to reintroduce that orphan to her heritage and history. The struggles and challenges that orphan possessed made going to that place impossible, but the love inspired by her life was there and speaking to the world. The improbability of events that led to that moment were nothing short of divine.

The circle had been epic. A boy raised in the traditions of religion and faith had ultimately sought escape from it through drive and tenacity. That ambition had birthed a song that foreshadowed the events of his own undoing in its own lines. Those lines had led to the financial fortune that would afford a transpacific adoption. That adoption would lead to a reluctant yet total surrender. That surrender would nurture the seeds of another song that would join a Chinese Angel and an American idol in the most unexpected of ways. That would bring redemption to a broken dreamer, go back across the Pacific, over the sands of Iwo Jima, into Beijing, and be transmitted all over the world and then gently land in the living room of one man and one woman raising a special little girl and a miraculous little boy.

No coincidence or accidents, but a beautiful art piece, deep, poetic, and pristine.

We watched, embraced, and cried. I had not known the song was going to be used for the Olympic games. No one from 19 had told me a thing. It was completely unexpected and totally out of the blue…as it should've been. Had my dreams come true in the way I had planned, I would've never been given that moment. I'm sure without the struggles and heartbreak, "Time of My Life" would've never been penned, at least not by me. If the chain of events had been any shorter in duration, I may have written it (or some watered down version of it) too early to have been sung by the right person at the right time, and it may have missed the Olympics altogether. Had I wallowed in my self-pity one more year and not listened to my wife (who I consider to have been an instrument of God in simply asking me to write the song and believing in me throughout the process), I would've surely missed the greatest example of God's faithfulness I've ever witnessed. In that one moment, watching the streets of Beijing, where I'd so casually promised to take my family five years earlier, filled with people in movement to the song inspired by one of their lost daughters, I felt as though God was pulling back the curtain of mystery and saying, "See, Regie? See what's back here? It's all okay. I have such beautiful things for everyone who believes and surrenders to my love, things you have not dreamed of. For I know the plans I have for you…plans to prosper you and not to harm you" (Jeremiah 29:11).

"Time of My Life" went on to close the Olympic games seven times during the two-week event. After the games were over, Oprah Winfrey declared it the "theme song of the 2008 Beijing Olympic Games" on her show. The song was used for several more finale shows that summer. It eventually went to number one on the Hot Adult Contemporary chart and reigned at number one for a record-breaking sixteen weeks on the Adult Contemporary chart, where it is the third longest-running number one song for a male artist in that chart's history. It went on to be downloaded over a million times and was on David Cook's debut CD that also sold over a million copies. It was the 2008 SESAC pop song of the year, and won Song of the Year at the Nashville Music Awards. The money earned by the song allowed me to get out of debt to the hospitals and the IRS. We finished the renovation of the relic and finally purchased a new car. When it was all said and done, one song had put me in a better place than I was before losing everything, before China, before children, before surrender. Everything I'd ever dreamed of happening for me as a songwriter happened, and more. But first I had to let it go.

You can't see that circle while you're making it, but it is happening in every random event and mundane movement. Our choices and chances are inextricably linked to a larger purpose whether we want to believe it or not. They say the chaos theory is based on a butterfly flapping its wings in China and changing the world. One insignificant event that sets off a chain reaction of events that ultimately effect us all. Maybe they're right. A butterfly in China certainly changed the world for me, but I don't believe it was chaos. I don't believe it was chance. I don't believe it was random. Sometimes you have to lose everything to gain perspective. Only at certain special moments can you pull back and see the reasons for it all. Only through surrender to something higher and greater can you ever truly experience the grand mosaic that is in a constant state of immaculate design.

SET IT ON FIRE

*A*nd so the road stretches out before me now, as it stretches before you. For me, the past, the future, ambition, music, artistic integrity, success, songwriting, money, fame, children, health, vitamins, nutrition, alcohol, faithlessness, despair, health care, physical disorders, sleep deprivation, dashed hopes, broken dreams, good intentions, self-centered actions, work ethic, chart-topping songs, achievement, Angelman Syndrome, adoption, family, identity—all of it, down to the core, has been placed on an altar of sorts. The same flesh and bone that once stood in defiance to the notion of surrender now embraces it daily, only because the spirit inside that flesh and bone has been changed. Sometimes God has to continually slap our hands and say, "No, no" in order to turn us into something more than we are, more than we were. Some of us are stubborn and insist we know what's best for ourselves. I tend to be one of those. I also tend to get taught lessons in such things time and time again.

I have no personal goal lists any more. I have no designs on new and exciting successes. I have nothing to prove. That's a good place to be. I also know that there are no random events, but all things are working together. Pip was indeed able to become a gentleman, but he was returned to himself in the end, as we all are. Can you achieve great things with great focus? Absolutely. Can you make your dreams come true? In this country, I still believe you can. Will those things fulfill you? Not a chance. Will they be the bedrock on which you can build your life? Never.

I'm not a preacher—I leave that to my father—but I am a seeker and someone who has attacked life with unrelenting fervor. Through those actions, I have been forced to become a student. What I've learned is that the ancient words of my father's sermons and my mother's songs were all true. I've learned that what the Apostle Paul said on Mars Hill in Acts chapter seventeen is a deep revelation. He told the Athenians, "The God you seek is not far from you." I stood on Mars Hill once while vacationing in Greece and was gently moved by those words and that story. Today, however, those words bring me to tears. "The God you seek is not far from you." "God is love" (1 John 4:8b, KJV). Love is truth; truth is God; God, again, is love. In the end, love is never far from us. Someone might say it's "as close as the beat of my heart."

While shooting photos for my latest music release, my longtime friend and photographer on the session, Devin Pense, was going through a difficult divorce and about to move to the West Coast. He had a setup idea for the shoot that involved getting an old piano, taking it to a field somewhere, and burning it. I loved it. We found an old upright online for a hundred bucks, bought it, and took it to a friend of mine's farm. We'd been shooting all day. Devin was leaving the next morning for his new life. Devin and I have been friends since we both dropped out of college. We were about to embark on a new chapter of friendship and new chapters in our lives. The last photo setup of the day was the burning piano. We placed fuel and fire starter logs in carefully chosen locations. We looked at each other; he lit the match. The piano started to burn. As he feverishly arranged lights and got the correct angles and shot picture after picture, and as I posed and played and worked with the flames licking at my hands, the old piano burned. As each ember turned to ash and sailed into the dark sky, I think Devin and I saw it as a kind of cleansing. The ironic metaphor of an old piano that had surely played thousands of sacred hymns, the kind of piano I could have very well played somewhere in my childhood, the kind of instrument that continually connected me to the past and the slavery of my obsessive ambition to pull away from it, the upright orthodoxy of correctness, stately craftsmanship, and work ethic, being stripped of its very music-making ability and then being cut in half and burned to the absolute ground was certainly not lost on me. As the piano burned, I chose to see it as a sacred sacrifice. I was offering up everything on an Old Testament-style altar of fire. My altar just happened to be a piano. I know we're not saved through such things. I know these are matters of the heart, but I have also learned that sometimes God gives you signs and moments of instruction and clarity. It's up to you to see them.

As the piano burned, I began singing a chorus. I didn't sing it as something that might someday be a hit song. I didn't try to sculpt it or shape it or make it into anything other than a prayer. As I travel the road laid out before me, I keep it close and know that it is a prayer from the purest place in my heart. My piano ultimately burned to the ground, so be it.

Every lie I've ever spoken
That left me bruised and broken
Every dream I thought would save me
Just a scar the cold world gave me
Every plan I hoped would lift me

That I just let shape and shift me
Every fear that keeps me tethered
To everything I've weathered
Set it on fire, set it on fire
In an ocean of flames 'til nothing remains
But you, but you
Set it on fire, set it on fire
Burn it down to the ground 'til nothing is found
But you, but you
Every demon, dark addiction
Every strong and stark affliction
All the past I've tried to carry
And the doubt I've tried to bury
All the pride I can't surrender
Like a rogue, repeat offender
Every wounded, weak emotion
Every faithless notion
Set it on fire, set it on fire
In an ocean of flames 'til nothing remains
But you, but you
Set it on fire, set it on fire
Burn it down to the ground 'til nothing is found
But you, but you
Burn away everything that keeps me in apathy
Burn away everything that keeps from running free
Set it on fire, set it on fire
In an ocean of flames 'til nothing remains
But you, but you
Set it on fire, set it on fire
Burn it down to the ground 'til nothing is found
But you, but you

set it on fire

REGIE HAMM

Also available from Regie Hamm

Set It On Fire
Featuring original hit single
"Time of My Life"
Available at www.tatemusicgroup.com and
everywhere music is sold.

How to get your free digital music download:

1. Visit www.tatepublishing.com and click on the
   e|LIVE logo on the home page.
2. Enter the following coupon code:
   e3c3-2891-5a0f-a74a-1a9f-ef2f-148b-a2f2
3. Download the music from your e|LIVE digital
   locker and begin enjoying your new digital entertainment package today!